where
DO I GO
from Here?

FINDING YOUR PERSONAL MISSION

AS A YOUNG ADULT WOMAN

IRENE ERICKSEN & JAN PINBOROUGH

BOOKCRAFT
SALT LAKE CITY, UTAH

BOOKCRAFT is a registered trademark of Deseret Book Company.

Visit us at deseretbook.com

Library of Congress Cataloging-in-Publication Data

Pinborough, Jan U.
    Where do I go from here? : finding your personal mission as a young adult woman / Jan U. Pinborough and Irene H. Ericksen.
    p.   cm.
    Includes bibliographical references and index.
    ISBN 1-57008-839-X (pbk.)
    1. Young women—Religious life.   2. Mormon women—Religious life.
I. Ericksen, Irene H.   II. Title.

BX8643.Y6 P56 2002
248.8'43'088283—dc21   2002006081

Printed in the United States of America   18961
R. R. Donnelley and Sons, Allentown, PA

10   9   8   7   6

For my mother, whose loving example

gave me my sense of self, and

for Dave, Alex, and Gerald,

whose love keeps me going.

—I.E.

For my mother, whose bright,

unfailing goodness has always

lit my path; and for my daughters,

who shine brighter day by day.

—J.P.

contents

contents

acknowledgments

I want to express my love and gratitude to my husband, Dave, for his support, his confidence in this book, and his crucial input. I gratefully recognize the mentoring and wisdom of the late Sister Maurine J. Turley, as well as the influence of Sister Ardeth G. Kapp and her general Young Women presidency and board. My deepest thanks go to Robert W. Raybould, for introducing me to the restored gospel. Finally, I acknowledge the loving hand of the Lord in my life and in the coming to fruition of this book.

—Irene Ericksen

I would like to thank my husband, Tom, without whose encouraging words and helpful deeds this book would have remained a dream; Elizabeth and Christiana, whose perceptive ideas guided me; and Susan Hainsworth, whose constant belief in this project kept me going. Most of all, I humbly acknowledge the Lord's blessing and enabling influence at every turn.

—Jan Pinborough

We would especially like to thank all of the "Lighting the Way" authors, who have been so generous in sharing their inspiring stories. We appreciate all the young adult women who told us about their lives and concerns and reacted to our ideas, especially Alexis, Becca, Brynn, Charlotte, Jane, Lindsay F., Lindsey R., Lisa, Lyndsay S., Sally, and Susie. We also appreciate Emily Watts' support and guidance, Janna DeVore's editing, and Tom Hewitson's beautiful design work.

introduction

WHERE'S THE MAP?

And I will bring [them] by a way that they knew not;

I will lead them in paths that they have not known:

I will make darkness light before them, and crooked things straight.

—Isaiah 42:16

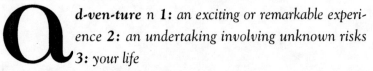

ad-ven-ture n **1**: *an exciting or remarkable experi-ence* **2**: *an undertaking involving unknown risks* **3**: *your life*

Every life is a grand adventure—a journey through the unknown. Of course, your journey *does* have a definite desti-nation—eternal life with God. But in between here and there lie great stretches of unfamiliar territory. And, if you are female, the journey holds a unique set of challenges.

For Latter-day Saint men, the path through young adult-hood is marked clearly, with signposts at major crossroads. As age nineteen approaches, for example, a prominent signpost reads, The Lord Wants You to Serve a Full-time Mission. Of course, young men must still decide whether or not to follow that signpost, but they *know* what the Lord wants them to do after high school. As they return from missions, young men see several other clear signposts: Finish Your Education, reads one. Establish a Career to Support a Family, reads another. Seek Out and Marry a Worthy Mate, reads yet another. While young men have to work out the details themselves, the frame-work for life is well-defined and, for the most part, under their control.

But for young adult Latter-day Saint women, the path is not so clearly marked. At many crossroads, there are questions instead of signposts: How much education should I pursue? Should I serve a full-time mission? Will I marry? If so, whom and when? If I marry, will I have children? Can I raise a family *and* have a career? What kind of career will be rewarding and allow me to support myself? Are there other purposes that Heavenly Father has for me in my life?

While this phase of life can be very exciting, it can also be confusing and overwhelming: What if I make a wrong turn?

Will I meet a dead end? Is there just one right path for me to find, or are there several equally good options? You may also have questions about what it means to be a woman, especially today, when some of the world's definitions seem to clash with the Lord's.

As you start making more of life's big decisions, you may become more aware of two facts: First, the journey you are on *really* matters. And, second, there's no map that shows exactly what lies ahead or which way to turn at each crossroads.

This book applies truths of the restored gospel to the challenges and decisions that are unique to young adult Latter-day Saint women. It also examines some of the troubling questions the world presents to you as you strive to live the gospel.

We hope that reading this book will help you mark your own path with a sense of purpose and with divine guidance. We hope it will help you to make decisions you will feel confident about and avoid some common problems that confront young women today. And above all, we hope it will help you make the contribution to God's work that only you can make—and that he needs you to make—at each point along your way. We wish for you his richest blessings on your journey.

Be strong and of a good courage, fear not, nor be afraid . . . :

for the Lord thy God, he it is that doth go with thee;

he will not fail thee, nor forsake thee.

—Deuteronomy 31:6

section 1

FINDING YOUR PATH

chapter 1

"FOR SUCH A TIME AS THIS"

There is neither man or woman in

this Church who is not on a mission.

That mission will last as long as they live.

—Brigham Young (JD, 12:394–95)

You have a mission. And it's not necessarily the go-to-the-MTC type. Even if your future seems unclear at the moment, one thing is certain. You have an absolutely unique personal mission—important things that Heavenly Father *needs* you to do and will *help* you to do. Your personal mission is not something optional. It is actually part of who you are, and learning to recognize it can guide you through the maze of decisions that lie before you now.

A mission long ago

Consider the life of a young woman who fulfilled her own unique mission long ago. Her name was Esther, and she was an obscure Jewish girl living in ancient Persia. Her parents had died, and she had been adopted by a relative. The Persian king, having divorced his wife for disobedience, had sent for all the beautiful young girls in the kingdom to be brought before him. He chose Esther as his queen, unaware that she was Jewish.

A few years after Esther's coronation, a high official in the Persian court convinced the king that the Jews were his enemies and had them condemned to extermination throughout the entire Persian empire. Esther knew that her people could be saved only if the king were to reverse his extermination decree. But under the harsh Persian law, the penalty for going uninvited before the king was death, and Esther had not been invited to appear before him.

How could Esther plead her people's case without losing her life? At the moment when she had to choose her course, Esther's adopted father, Mordecai, asked her a crucial question: "Who knoweth whether thou art come to the kingdom for such a time as this?" (Esther 4:14).

Fearful and uncertain of her own ability to do what was required of her, Esther asked her people to join her in fasting. Then, taking her life in her hands, she went to the king, who heard her petition and reversed the extermination decree. The young Israelite woman had saved her people, and with them the records and traditions of the house of Israel.

Think of Esther's mission as the intersection of three elements:

> **1. Esther's gifts.** Esther had great personal gifts—strength of character, mental quickness, courage, and exceptional physical beauty. Her circumstances also gave her some unusual opportunities. She was married to the king of the Persian empire and thus found herself in a unique position to have access to the most powerful man in the Middle East.
>
> **2. Esther's challenges.** Esther had personal weaknesses, too. She lacked confidence and had doubts and fears. Her circumstances were unusually challenging. Orphaned and forced to marry out of her faith, she lived in a world ruled totally by men and was a Jew living in an empire ruled by the enemies of her people.
>
> **3. The needs in her world and what God needed Esther to do.** The Jewish people had been condemned to death, and God needed Esther to use her unique gifts and challenges—with his help—to save them.

Your Gifts, Your Challenges, Your World

"I've heard this all before," you might think. "But *my* life doesn't seem so important. Even if *I* do have something special to accomplish on earth, how will I know if I'm fulfilling it?"

Your personal mission is not something mystical and elusive. It is not something "out there" far in the future that you will find only if you don't make any missteps. Actually, you can think of your personal mission as a combination of three things you already have:

1. Your gifts. These include your personal strengths—your natural talents and abilities—as well as the positive opportunities your unique circumstances offer you. These are raw materials that you will use in fulfilling your personal mission.

2. Your challenges. These include your personal weaknesses, as well as the seemingly negative or limiting aspects of your circumstances. These, too, are a unique part of who you are, and they will play an important role in your personal mission.

3. The needs in your world and what God needs you to do about them. The needs in your world are many—from the global to those nearest at hand—and God *needs* you to make your unique contribution in meeting them.

"A work that no other can do"

At the moment when the survival of the Jewish people hung in the balance, Esther was in a position to do something that literally no other person on earth could do. Is it possible that at this moment you and your generation stand at a pivotal point in the survival of God's children? In these times of worsening social problems, could it be that young Latter-day Saint women are—like Esther—in a crucial position of influence? A prophet of God, President Ezra Taft Benson, seemed to answer this question when he said, "You have been born at this time for a sacred and glorious purpose. It is not by chance that you have been reserved to come to earth in this last dispensation of the fulness of times. . . . You are to be the royal daughters of the Lord in the last days" ("To the Young Women of the Church," 81).

Perhaps it is true that, just as a courageous young girl saved the ancient Jewish people, young women today have significant, even world-saving, missions to fulfill. Perhaps it could be asked of each young Latter-day Saint woman, "Who knows whether you have been born on earth for such a time as this?"

Dare to do right! Dare to be true! You have a work that no other can do.
—George L. Taylor (*Children's Songbook,* 158)

Lighting the way

IF I DIDN'T TRY, WHO WOULD?

NATALIA YERESKOVSKA

Growing up in Cherkassy, Ukraine, I had never heard of The Church of Jesus Christ of Latter-day Saints. In fact, my parents wanted me to be an atheist. But deep in my heart, I always felt there was a Supreme Being who loved me and wanted me to find the truth about him. I searched out various religions, finding many wonderful things in their doctrines, but feeling that something was missing in each one. Still, I continued my search, praying to God for guidance.

When I was fifteen years old, I applied and was accepted as an exchange student in the United States for the 1995–96 school year. I hoped that somehow I would be assigned to a religious family. Meanwhile, in Chicago, Brother Bruce and Sister Jean Bingham were praying and fasting about their choice of an exchange student, and they felt strongly impressed to select me.

When I arrived in Chicago, I told my host family, "It is not by chance that I am here. God sent me to you." When I learned that my new family strongly believed in God and Jesus Christ, I was thrilled and felt impressed to learn more about their religious beliefs. So every Sunday I went with the Binghams to sacrament meetings, and every weekday I went to early-morning seminary. I loved attending Young Women activities, as well as family scripture studies, home evenings, and family prayers. And the more I learned, the more I felt like the pieces of a huge puzzle were beginning to come together.

Eventually, I asked for missionaries so that I could learn even more. After fasting and prayer, I received a powerful testimony that pierced my whole being with the knowledge that The Church of Jesus Christ of Latter-day Saints is indeed true. Miraculously, my parents granted permission for me to be baptized, and my dream came true. I was baptized into the true Church I had been longing to find.

Several months later, I sat on the return flight to Ukraine, overwhelmed with doubts and fears. In my entire city of over 350,000 people, I was going to be the only Latter-day Saint. I did not know when I would ever have another opportunity to partake of the sacrament and share the joy of the gospel with others of my faith. Every night I prayed for the Lord to support me in my lonely hours.

Just a few weeks after I returned home, Kiev mission president Wilfried Voge invited me to Kiev for the national LDS youth conference. There I met Brother Ted Gashler, a Church member who had hosted a professor from Cherkassy in his home in the United States. "Professor Morozov never joined the Church," Brother Gashler said, "but he might help with the permission to proselyte in your city." President Voge had not planned to open Cherkassy for missionary work for a while, but he now felt prompted to do so as soon as possible. Legally, missionaries could not come to Cherkassy until an adult resident of the city wrote a letter officially inviting them to come. And a branch could not be established without a request signed by a number of Cherkassy residents.

I was only sixteen years old and did not feel adequate to accomplish such a task. But I was the only Church member in

Cherkassy. If *I* didn't try, who would? I arranged to meet Professor Morozov. As we talked about America and the Church, to my surprise he said, "I am so disturbed that my students are wasting their precious years on drugs, smoking, alcohol, and sleeping around. Let's start the LDS church in our town. Our youth are Ukraine's future, and this could help turn them back in a positive direction." I explained to him the required steps, and Professor Morozov gladly agreed to help. Moreover, he invited missionaries to speak to his students.

Soon after that conversation, I felt prompted to ask the head counselor of my school to invite the missionaries, too. "Our school could benefit from native English speakers, while they teach our people their Christian belief," I told her. Mrs. Ananyeva agreed to write an invitation to the missionaries, and even invited them to speak to her students and, eventually, to teach English as volunteers.

In October 1996, the first missionaries of The Church of Jesus Christ of Latter-day Saints arrived in Cherkassy. Because we did not have a building, we held our first meeting on a windy beach. About eight of us, standing in the cold, facing the wind, sang "Come, Come, Ye Saints" and spoke about service. The next week Elder F. Enzio Busche of the Quorum of Seventy came to speak to us, and about twenty curious people came to listen. By January, the missionaries had baptized Professor Morozov's wife, his daughter, and son-in-law. More baptisms followed, and more missionaries. Young Women, Relief Society, Primary, and Sunday School groups were organized. Priesthood holders were ordained. A branch president was called. Two of my lifelong friends were baptized. Some families went to the temple in Germany and were sealed for eternity. The Church was established in Cherkassy, Ukraine.

Looking back, I marvel at how the Lord opened the way for something that seemed impossible to come to pass. For months I had cried every night for help, seeing only an obscure vision of the branch in Cherkassy. But the Lord heard my prayers and with our efforts made it happen.

The Lord has continued to open the way in my life. After high school, I enrolled at Brigham Young University, where I am studying international law and diplomacy. During the summer of 2000, I had the opportunity to return to Ukraine with a group of BYU volunteers. There we were able to help in establishing the first Center for Religious Freedom and Information of its kind in Ukraine. We did translation, research, fundraising, and conducted a public campaign against smoking. While I was there, I once again attended the Cherkassy Branch, which now has its own chapel and piano.

Recently I again saw God's hand in my life. During the 2002 Paralympics in Salt Lake City, I attended a luncheon for the first lady of Ukraine, who was visiting Utah during the Olympics. Before lunch I had placed my jacket on a chair at the table where I was planning to sit. When I returned to sit down I found that someone else was sitting in my chair. A man across the table noticed my confusion and kindly invited me to sit in an unoccupied seat next to his. He was Dr. Thomas Griffith, the general counsel at BYU. During lunch he told me about a project he was helping with—an American Bar Association initiative to improve justice, human rights, and law enforcement in Eastern and Central Europe. Because of my "accidental" meeting that day, I was invited to serve an internship with that organization this summer.

Today, I need the assurance that God will guide me as much as I ever have before. Recently I have applied for admission to eight respected law schools in the United States, and so far, I have received two rejections. This is a big trial of my faith, but I keep remembering that God is mindful of me and will make sure I don't get lost, no matter what happens. As President Hinckley has said, when we put forth our best effort, trusting in the Lord, "God will always make a way where there is no way. Of this I am assured" ("God Will Make a Way," *New Era*, January 2002, 6).

NATALIA YERESKOVSKA ENJOYS POETRY, SINGING, PLAYING THE PIANO AND UKRAINIAN FLUTE, TENNIS, BASKETBALL, DANCE, AND INTERNATIONAL POLITICS. SHE IS A GRADUATE OF BRIGHAM YOUNG UNIVERSITY AND WILL BEGIN LAW SCHOOL IN FALL 2002. NATALIA'S GRANDPARENTS HAVE HAD THE MISSIONARY DISCUSSIONS, AND HER PARENTS HAVE HOSTED THE MISSIONARIES. "I HOPE THAT ONE DAY THEY WILL BE UNITED WITH ME IN THE TEMPLE FOR ETERNITY," SAYS NATALIA.

And thus we see that by small means
the Lord can bring about great things.
—1 Nephi 16:29

chapter 2

Your Gifts:
Fitted to Your Mission

These are your presents, . . . and they are tools not toys.

The time to use them is perhaps near at hand. Bear them well.

—Aslan (in Lewis, *Lion, Witch, and Wardrobe*, 117–18)

I n fairy tales, one who undertakes an important quest receives special gifts to help her successfully complete her mission. Dorothy in *The Wizard of Oz* is given a pair of ruby slippers. Ella, of the updated Cinderella tale *Ella Enchanted*, receives her mother's necklace and a magical book. In C. S. Lewis's children's classic *The Lion, the Witch, and the Wardrobe*, Susan is given a bow with arrows and a horn with which to summon divine help, and Lucy a diamond dagger and a healing medicine.

These fairy tales echo deep realities. It is not hard to picture our Heavenly Parents presenting to each daughter departing for her dangerous mortal quest a carefully selected set of gifts. In truth, you *do* have special divinely bestowed gifts, and they are precisely fitted to the journey before you.

What powerful gifts did you bring with you from your premortal life? You may not yet recognize some of these gifts—even some of the most essential. Unfortunately, young women are often more familiar with their weaknesses than with their gifts. Most carry around a mental list of physical characteristics they wish they could change: "I'm ten pounds too heavy. My complexion is bad. My nose is too big." Most, too, also have a ready list of other personal weaknesses. "I'm shy. I'm not athletic. I'm not very talented." But in fact, you have many gifts that you do not yet recognize. And your mission will require you to recognize and use these gifts God has given you.

Taking stock: The first step

To do this, begin by taking stock of your set of gifts and abilities. You will need to pay attention to your talents and strengths of spirit and personality. You will need to notice the unique gifts that you have because you are a woman. You will need to become more aware of your dreams and desires.

What do you like to do? What do you think you are good at? What do people tell you you are good at? These are clues to the gifts God has given you. As you look at the following lists, think about what talents and traits seem to come naturally to you. Recall compliments you have received from others. Then make a check by the traits you think you may have—even in a small degree. Add others that are not listed. Then, as your awareness grows over the coming months and years, add more checks. Return to these lists to lift your vision on days when you are feeling discouraged or uninspired.

Talents and Abilities

Most of us will never play soccer like Mia Hamm or sing like Celine Dion. Few of us will go to Harvard or play in the WNBA or have a painting hanging in the Metropolitan Museum of Art. Unfortunately, we sometimes recognize only those who are extremely gifted as having talents. Sometimes we may even feel that we have talent only if we qualify for an athletic team or win a prize. But a lack of external validation does not mean we have no talent in that area. The fact that on a given day you don't make the team, for example, does not diminish the fact that you have athletic talent. You may still have the talent, and it is meant to bless your life.

Even worse, we often recognize only certain kinds of abilities—such as musical, artistic, or athletic ones—as talents. So when many of us count our talents, we count ourselves out. But many of the talents society values least—as measured by the money and prestige they earn—are actually among the most valuable. For example, a gifted teacher or an encouraging friend often contributes more to the world than a supermodel does.

Recognizing your talents is not arrogant. In fact, how can you express gratitude to God for giving you these remarkable gifts unless you recognize them? As you read the list below, do not be afraid to acknowledge even talents that you only suspect you might have. If you place a check mark by them, you may be surprised at the count when you're done:

____ spontaneous	____ organized
____ good at making things	____ generous
____ good listener	____ creative
____ good sense of humor	____ optimistic
____ thoughtful	____ good teacher
____ good with children	____ responsible
____ neat and tidy	____ sensitive to others' feelings
____ good friend	____ hard worker
____ artistic (enjoy or are good at art)	____ musical (enjoy or are good at music)
____ not critical of others	____ good communicator
____ athletic (enjoy or are good at sports)	____ committed to doing your best
____ helpful	____ loyal
____ patient	____ good at math
____ love to read	____ good cook
____ good writer	____ honest
____ enthusiastic	____ make others feel good

Others: _____

_____

_____

_____

Women's Gifts

A special inheritance of gifts is part of your divine female nature as a daughter of Heavenly Parents. While not every woman has all of these gifts, they form a common pattern that can be seen across womankind.

The gift of mothering/nurturing. The hallmark of women's gifts is that of giving and nurturing life and caring for people. We were divinely designed to be capable of and interested in doing this. Only women give physical life to babies. Our bodies are curved and soft so that we can cradle and comfort children—both our own and those of others. We have been programmed biologically to perceive an infant's needs and respond to their cries. Women's brains are specially structured to be skilled in the use of language, the perception and expression of emotion, and the capacity for empathy. Thus, we are gifted in communicating, building relationships, and responding to human needs—whether of our own loved ones or of others in need of mothering. Historically, women have spearheaded some of the great movements of social compassion, from prison reform to the abolition of slavery, striving to relieve human suffering in its many forms.

The gift of civilizing. We use our creativity and our intellect to improve our communities and to beautify our surroundings. We build connections between neighbors. We band together for good causes and are courageous in defending right and virtue. In ways large and small, women help to civilize the world.

Women have done this through the centuries by their manner of behavior. Historically, women have been the custodians of characteristics of gentleness and courtesy, of sweetness and of gracious influence. These qualities tame the savage beast in all of humanity, and without them the world would be a cold and hostile place. However, this womanly ideal seems less valued in our modern culture, as so many popular female icons exemplify a style that is outspoken, aggressive, and coarse. Yet women do not have to be loud and pushy to be strong. The world badly needs the quiet strength and refining influence of women who are at peace with this side of their nature and are not afraid to be kind, gentle, and supportive in their manner.

The gift of spiritual strength. Women's spirits are both sensitive and fervent. We are strongly committed to principle and full of faith. We strive to be in tune with spiritual promptings.

The gift of endurance. Women also have other strengths of body and spirit. We are physically hardy, living on average longer than men. We also have a capacity to be emotionally strong, patient, and long-suffering, especially with those we love.

One very important part of your mission is to recognize and use your remarkable feminine strengths. See if you can identify the seeds of any of these gifts within your female character:

____ good at communicating

____ peacemaking

____ drawn to nurturing others

____ courageous in defending right

____ good at building relationships

____ full of compassion for the downtrodden

____ morally upright

____ sensitive to spiritual things

____ loyal to loved ones

____ physically hardy

____ inclined to make things beautiful

____ caring for and about children

____ sensitive to others' feelings and needs

____ intuitive

Divine Attributes and Spiritual Gifts

Your divine attributes are traits that you have literally inherited from your Heavenly Parents—just as you may have inherited blue eyes or an outgoing personality from your earthly parents. Some of these attributes are in embryonic form right now, but they will grow throughout your life. Your spiritual gifts are special strengths of spirit that God has given you, or may give you, as you earnestly seek them to bless his children (see D&C 46:8, 26). Your patriarchal blessing can give you clues about which ones you have. You may want to indicate those, as well as the spiritual gifts you *desire* to have, on the list below:

_____ loving	_____ able to discern truth
_____ truthful	_____ gracious
_____ forgiving	_____ creative
_____ slow to anger	_____ virtuous
_____ striving for goodness	_____ patient
_____dependable	_____ kind
_____ charitable	_____ possessing knowledge
_____ wise	_____ able to teach
_____ strong in testimony	_____ having faith to be healed
_____ able to receive personal revelation	_____ able to learn and understand languages
_____ a believer in the of power of miracles	_____ able to discern the presence angels
_____ having faith in the testimony of others	_____ having faith in Christ

Dreams and Desires

Your righteous dreams and desires are another kind of gift. They give you emotional fuel to propel you forward. You probably have at least a few well-formed dreams. You may dream of traveling to exciting places or working in a certain career or marrying a certain kind of person. But you probably also have many other less well-defined yearnings. Perhaps you feel you would really like to do something worthwhile, though you don't know right now what that might be.

Take the time to pay attention to, and nurture, your righteous desires and your dreams for the future. Some of the specifics of your future life may not exactly match your dreams. Still, you will grow in the direction of your righteous desires. And your dreams and desires will help guide you in fulfilling your mission.

Some of my dreams and desires:

_____

_____

_____

_____

_____

_____

Favorable Circumstances

Your gifts also include the favorable circumstances in your life. You live in a time when many women in the modern world have opportunities for education, for example. Perhaps your life has been free of serious financial hardship. You may be blessed to have grown up in a loving home or to be part of a supportive extended family. You may live in a nation that provides safety and opportunity to its citizens. Maybe you have a family who tries to live the gospel. Or maybe you have had an influential leader who has helped you stay close to the Church. Writing down the favorable circumstances in your life can be a powerful way to take stock of your position in the world.

_____

_____

_____

_____

_____

_____

uniquely yours

You may feel tempted to compare your set of gifts with someone else's. But comparing will make you feel proud and superior to some people, envious and inferior to others. Your set of talents, abilities, and personal strengths is like no one else's. And these gifts are meant to be used to help others. As the Lord explained, "For all have not every gift given unto them; for there are many gifts, and to every [woman] is given a gift by the Spirit of God. To some is given one, and to some is given another, that all may be profited thereby" (D&C 46:11–12).

As you focus on recognizing and using what *you* have been given, you will feel more secure and have greater energy to use these gifts as the Lord intends.

Behold thou hast a gift. . . .

Remember it is sacred and cometh from above.

—Doctrine and Covenants 6:10

WHILE I FOUND MY GIFTS, MY MISSION FOUND ME

CELIA BAKER

During my growing-up years, I had a passionate love for music and knowledge. I spent countless hours at the piano—practicing, improvising and composing, or just playing songs. I read good books and wrote elaborate journals. I had a strong feeling that these were gifts the Lord meant for me to use.

As I grew older, I began to realize that my talents were more the ordinary kind: I wasn't destined to be another Mozart or to write a great literary work. Further, I became aware that the remoteness of my home in southeastern Utah had limited my opportunities for instruction. When I entered college, I made the painful discovery that I was hopelessly behind my classmates in some areas of my musical background. I was only a so-so writer and a fair-to-middling pianist with an unmagnificent singing voice. Still, my heart was full of desire to make music and to write. It was during this eye-opening period of discouragement that I began to understand my real gifts and how the Lord intended for me to use them.

While I was still in high school, my bishop had asked me to be the Sunday School chorister, which meant I would direct the entire ward in weekly hymn practice. This made me feel embarrassed and inadequate at the time. I had never conducted music, and I was afraid the other teenagers in the ward would laugh at me when I tried to create enthusiasm for the hymns. I talked to my father about my feelings, and he advised me that great opportunities are often hard to recognize. They come disguised, he said, as tasks we are afraid to try, or as plain old hard work. He left it up to me to decide what to tell the bishop but counseled that when chances to use or develop our skills come along, the best answer is usually "yes."

Over the years I have said "yes" to many opportunities, and each has brought other opportunities, more chances for growth, and moments when my life's mission has come into sharper focus. I have discovered that the Lord values steady workers who love what they do, and that much can be accomplished when modest talents are applied with consistent effort. My Father in Heaven never intended for me to be a concert pianist or to write the great American novel. My mission is broader and more personal than that. It encompasses my sacred calling as a mother, my church service, and contributions to community and career that I would never have imagined in my youth.

The spiritual gift of a willing heart—a type of faith in self and in God—is the gift I am most grateful for. Because I have been willing to try new things, risk ridicule, and share my skills with others, my ordinary-sized talents have grown sufficient for the service the Lord needs from me. In this gradual way, I began to recognize that an important aspect of my mission was to be a *teacher* of music, rather than a performer or composer as I originally envisioned.

When my three daughters were very young, I taught private music lessons at home. As my daughters grew to school age, I became a public schoolteacher, keeping the same schedule as theirs. My long-ago experience as Sunday School chorister helped me discover a great love for conducting choral music. As a teacher, I built a large choral music program and a sweet-voiced children's choir that included my daughters. I took particular joy in providing my students with some of the educational experiences I had missed in my youth. My own experience made me sensitive to the abilities of others, and I was able to help many young people believe in and develop their talents.

My dreams of being an author have also taken a turn I did not expect. As my children grew older, an unexpected opportunity to write free-lance articles about music for a newspaper came my way. Again, I felt inadequate and almost said no. I'm glad I said yes instead. That little opportunity grew into an exciting new career as an arts journalist. This has allowed me to combine both of my loves of music and writing.

As I direct one more stake choir, help one more teenager prepare for a music festival, write one more article, or play the organ at one more church meeting, I look around. I am surrounded by amazing women—one planning magnificent ward banquets and running a catering business with the help of her children, another presiding over the Primary and working quietly for worthy political causes, another making beautiful items for her home and for others, while another immerses herself in humanitarian service. There was a time when none of these women knew where or how the Lord wanted her to serve, just as I did not know. It wasn't so hard to find his will. We simply got busy, and our missions found us.

CELIA R. BAKER IS A JOURNALIST, MUSICIAN, AND EDUCATOR WHO
RESIDES IN CENTERVILLE, UTAH, WHERE SHE CONDUCTS HER WARD CHOIR
AND IS WARD ORGANIST. SHE AND HER HUSBAND, WALTER L. BAKER, ARE
THE PARENTS OF THREE DAUGHTERS.

Neglect not the gift that is in thee.

—1 Timothy 4:14

chapter 3

YOUR CHALLENGES: ROCKS OR JEWELS?

"Good morrow to you, my good lass,"
[Rumpelstiltskin said]. "What are you weeping for?"
"Alas," answered she, "I must spin this straw
into gold, and I know not how."
—The Brothers Grimm (*Fairy Tales*, 165)

Imagine that you are walking barefoot along the warm beach and stub your toe on something hard in the sand. Using your hands, you start digging. Soon the outlines of a wooden box appear. Amazed, you see that it looks just like a pirate's treasure chest, right out of an old movie. Could it really be a chest of pirate's treasure? You excitedly brush the sand off the top and raise the lid on its rusty hinges. Your heart sinks. This is not a box full of gleaming jewels and gold. It's nothing but a worthless bunch of rocks. Disgusted, you set it back down and start to lower the lid. . . .

A BOX OF ROCKS

Every life has its own "box of rocks"—characteristics and circumstances that seem worthless, and even damaging to us. Some of these are personality traits—perhaps a quick temper, shyness, or a tendency to feel depressed. Some are physical weaknesses—ranging from a feeling of unattractiveness to serious illnesses and debilitating handicaps. Some are intellectual weaknesses, such as problems with reading or mathematics. And all of us face trying circumstances. Your parents may be divorced or unhappily married. You may have experienced the death of a parent, sibling, or close friend. Maybe a close family member is abusive or an alcoholic. You may be the only Church member in your family—or the only one trying to live the gospel.

But, unlike the box on the beach, you cannot simply walk away from these "rocks" if you choose. This box—with all of its unwanted contents—is part of you.

Meanwhile, back on the beach, . . . just as you start to lower the lid on the box, you see a glint of red. Picking up one of the small dirt-encrusted objects and scraping at the dirt, you find what appears to be a large ruby. It needs polishing, but its clarity and beauty are evident. Quickly cleaning off another "rock," you find a sparkling sapphire. You pick up one of the smallest rocks in your box, wondering what it might be. To your amazement, it appears to be an uncut diamond, a literal diamond in the rough.

You realize that the contents of this box can change your life. These jewels will open up options you would not otherwise have— education, travel, helping others in serious need. All of these exciting possibilities will now be yours—but only because you looked beyond the dirty surfaces to find what was hidden beneath.

Another Kind of Gift

Is it possible that your weaknesses—even the ones that plague you most—could eventually be of great value to you? Could your challenges—like the straw that the miller's daughter in "Rumpelstiltskin" spun into gold—actually be gifts in disguise?

The Lord has promised that it can be so—if we turn to him in humility. "And if [women] come unto me I will show unto them their weakness. I give unto [women] weakness that they may be humble; and my grace is sufficient for all [women] that humble themselves before me; for if they humble themselves before me, . . . then will I make weak things become strong unto them" (Ether 12:27). Only the Lord knows how to help you spin the straw in your life into gold, and he is waiting to show you how.

Besides keeping us from being arrogant, our challenges serve other important purposes. If she had not been blind and deaf, could Helen Keller have written so movingly about the beauties of the world? If Sister Sheri Dew were not single, would she be able to speak so compellingly to other women whose lives have not fit the expected pattern? Without the gravelly whisper that resulted from throat cancer, would the voice of President Spencer W. Kimball have conveyed such faith in the face of adversity?

Like the challenges of each of these great people, your challenges and weaknesses are actually a crucial part of who you are. And you will be able to fulfill your particular mission not just *in spite* of them, but also *because* of them. A girl who struggles to learn to read may grow up to be an especially gifted and understanding teacher. A very shy young woman may become a sensitive writer and compassionate friend. A student who has to work hard to do well in school can develop a very strong character that will eventually lead to success.

Try this: List some of your challenges below, in the column to the left. To the right of each one, describe ways this challenge could actually become a strength to you.

_____   _____

                                      _____

                                      _____

_____   _____

                                      _____

_____   _____

_____

_____

_____   _____

_____

_____

_____   _____

_____

_____   _____

_____

_____

_____   _____

_____

_____

framing your life with faith

Of course, our challenges are not transformed into strengths overnight. It may take many years of struggling with certain challenges before the blessings will emerge. The purposes of a few of the most difficult challenges may not even become apparent until the next life. In the meantime, it is vital not to let our weaknesses and challenges dominate our view of ourselves.

If you pick up a very small rock and hold it very close to your eye, you can block out your view of the whole glorious world. A tiny rock can even obscure the sun, which is billions of times larger! Likewise, by focusing too much on your weaknesses and challenges, you can lose sight of the many, much larger gifts and blessings of your life.

What sets a master photographer apart from the person who merely takes pictures? In part, it is the ability to frame the subject. Imagine that a professional photographer and an amateur were sent out to take photographs in a beautiful wildlife refuge. The photographer's work would show striking shots of places and animals. But the amateur's might show mountains with the tops cut off and other carelessly composed photographs. You, too, can become like a master photographer when you focus on the blessings in your own life—not denying the difficulties but choosing to place in the center of each frame the positive parts of your life.

As a well-known hymn teaches, when life's difficulties overwhelm you, a great way to counteract worry and anxiety is to simply "count your blessings; name them one by one" (*Hymns*, no. 241). If you have never done this by writing them down on paper, you may be surprised at the change this can make in your point of view. Another tactic that can be equally powerful is to count other people's challenges. See how many people you know who are carrying significant burdens. Writing down each person's name and the trial he or she is experiencing can create quite a humbling list.

"Thread by Thread"

However, even after taking these steps to keep things in perspective, you may still feel like some things in your life will never work out. If you are struggling with feelings of genuine heartache or hopelessness, "counting your blessings" may seem like a trite response.

If you regularly experience debilitating feelings of sadness or hopelessness, you may need to take steps beyond the important one of accentuating the positive. You may be experiencing clinical depression, a medical condition that causes life to seem bleak or full of despair. You can consult with your bishop, LDS Family Services, a school counselor, or a physician to find out if professional help is needed in your situation. Depression and other conditions, such as anxiety disorders, panic attacks, bipolar disorder, and obsessive-compulsive disorder, can require professional attention. These conditions can be caused by your biochemistry as well as by your life circumstances and emotional makeup. The many effective medical and psychological treatments for these conditions are among the blessings of modern science, just as insulin is a great blessing to diabetics.

As you take steps to cope positively with your challenges, you can be sure that the Lord understands your weaknesses and loves you—even while you still have them. "For God sent not his Son into the world to condemn the world; but that the world through him might be saved" (John 3:17). One of the ways that Christ saves us on a daily basis occurs when we come unto him and admit our weaknesses so that he can make us strong (see Ether 12:27).

This process of dealing with weaknesses is a very precious part of your personal mission, and you cannot fulfill your mission without it. Striving to triumph over your weaknesses and challenges can build humility, empathy, and strength. When you seek God's help in your struggle, you will also become more aware of his miraculous power in your life.

Your life is like a tapestry that must be sewn thread by thread for thousands of hours before the beautiful pattern is visible. As you patiently work through losses, setbacks, and

seeming defeats, the whole pattern of your life will eventually emerge as a thing of wondrous beauty. Over a lifetime, you will see great challenges become great blessings.

Got any rivers you think are uncrossable?

Got any mountains you can't tunnel through?

God specializes in things thought impossible.

He does the things others cannot do.

—"Got Any Rivers" (*Making Melody*, no. 111)

"More Used Would I Be"

Jan Pinborough

My college years were filled with growth, fun, and new experiences. They were also filled with deep insecurities and even torment. While I was enjoying my wonderful roommates and loving my BYU student ward, I was also painfully shy and not dating. Much more agonizing, though, was the fact that my parents' marital difficulties were reaching a crescendo that I could sense a thousand miles away over the phone lines. Sick at heart, I didn't want to admit to myself what I secretly felt—that my family was not going to be eternal after all.

One night, looking for some kind of peace, I parked my old blue Volkswagen outside the Provo Temple and tried to frame a prayer more specific than "Please help me." The temple was resplendently gold and white against the midnight blue sky. As its beauty sank into me, another simple plea came to my mind: "More used would I be." It was actually a line from a favorite hymn, and as I repeated it in my mind, I realized that this truly was my deepest desire—to be a willing instrument in the Lord's hands.

Since that night long ago, this often-repeated prayer has guided me along a very fulfilling path. And I have learned that the Lord has been able to use my weaknesses, as well as my strengths, for his purposes. Because I was socially awkward, and also because I feared having a disastrous marriage, I did not marry until I was in my thirties. While this was difficult in itself, during this time I was able to earn two college degrees, polishing my writing skills in the process.

When I was offered an internship as an editor for the Church, my prayer to be able to use my abilities for Him guided me to accept the job.

For many years now I have edited and written manuals, articles, and songs for Church members—first full time, then part time, and now freelance. And in all my work, my background as an extremely shy girl from a very troubled home has served me well. When I edited a Primary lesson on families, for example, I was able to add the perspective of children whose homes were less than ideal. When I was assigned to write a series of articles on disabilities, I could do it with greater compassion and sensitivity than I might have otherwise. And most satisfying of all, I was able to write an article to encourage youth from deeply troubled families like mine.

In my home today, I have two handmade gifts. One is a large quilt made from dozens of colorful fabrics by a master quilt maker. The other is a small bird-shaped pincushion stitched from a few scraps of felt by a good friend. Even though one of these gifts was made with many materials and a high level of skill, and the other with few materials and more basic skills, I would be hard-pressed to say which is dearer to me or which has brought me greater pleasure. In other words, no matter how few talents and abilities we start out with in life, and no matter how many weaknesses and limitations we have, each of us has enough to make something beautiful and pleasing to the Lord.

How grateful I am that God has been able to use my

strengths *and* my weaknesses, answering my simple prayer in a far more wonderful way than I ever could have imagined.

I know that he will do the same for you.

JAN PINBOROUGH GREW UP IN MIDLAND, TEXAS. SHE GRADUATED FROM BRIGHAM YOUNG UNIVERSITY WITH A BACHELOR'S DEGREE IN ENGLISH AND A MASTER'S DEGREE IN TEACHING ENGLISH AS A SECOND LANGUAGE. A FREE-LANCE EDITOR AND WRITER, SHE AND HER HUSBAND, THOMAS PINBOROUGH, LIVE WITH THEIR TWO DAUGHTERS IN SALT LAKE CITY. SHE ENJOYS LITERATURE, MUSIC, AND QUILTING AND SERVES AS A WARD PRIMARY PRESIDENT.

If they . . . have faith in me, then will I make

weak things become strong unto them.

—Ether 12:27

chapter 4

Your Mission:
What God Needs *You* to Do

Between now and the day the Lord comes again,

He needs women . . . in every nation who

will step forward in righteousness and say by their words

and their actions, "Here am I, send me."

—M. Russell Ballard (in *Bear Record of Me,* 322–23)

So when and where does *your* mission begin? You may think it lies in some distant time or place. But it actually begins right now, right where you are. At any given moment, there are many, many needs in your world. You have the set of gifts and resources needed to help fill some of them. And *that* point—wherever a need intersects with your ability to fill it—is where your mission is found.

The Needs in Your World

Different moments in history require different heroic responses from God's children. Under Moses' direction, the Israelites left the security of Egyptian civilization for a harsh trek into an unknown land. The two thousand stripling warriors in the Book of Mormon risked their lives in battle to save their people. Early Saints left their homes in Nauvoo, endured the bitter cold of Winter Quarters, and followed a prophet to an unknown and barren land to build a temple of the Lord and establish his church. In our modern day, the Sisters of Charity, founded by Mother Theresa, give food, medical care, and love to some of the world's most destitute and desperate people.

It's easy to see the "great thing" that each of these groups has done. What "great thing" might your generation of young adult women be needed to do? And what "heroic responses" might be required? Consider these possibilities.

Stand as a witness for the Savior and his church
• By sharing your faith with others.
• By standing up for Christian virtues, such as honesty, kindness, civility, and goodness.
• By being unashamed of your standards and values as a member of his church.

Stand up for womanhood in our society

• By being glad to be a woman and not ashamed of traditionally feminine strengths and virtues.

• By your personal choices in clothing and entertainment, refusing to support indecency and the degradation of the female body.

Help save the coming generation of children

• By standing up for the work of mothering and home-building.

• By preparing to be a full-time mother if you have the opportunity.

• By filling voids in "mothering" by nurturing others' children wherever you find the need.

• By looking for ways to respond to the needs of at-risk children in your community and impoverished childrren throughout the world.

• By supporting and defending families.

• By working to prevent teenage pregnancy and unwed parenthood.

Help clean up our culture

• By becoming involved in public policy that upholds standards of public morality and fights pornography and the sexual exploitation of women (for example, making telephone calls to advertisers, supporting beneficial laws).

• By speaking up at school and at work, in courteous and kind ways, for righteous standards of behavior and speech.

• By taking a stand *for* what is wholesome, and *against* profanity, vulgarity, and violence.

Look for opportunities to serve the needs of the poor and downtrodden in your community and the larger world

•By volunteering your services to humanitarian groups.

•By organizing service projects that fill needs of the impoverished, the elderly, or disadvantaged.

•By becoming politically active in your community.

What other great needs do you see in your world? What are some ways you could address them?

Your generation of young adult women is uniquely positioned to make a difference because so many of the assaults on the family and morality in our world today are aimed directly at you! The adversary knows that young women are pivotal and that in many ways the well-being of the next generation depends on the decisions and responses you make to his assaults. The Lord needs today's young women to draw a line in the sand and hold strongly to it.

Inspiration and Initiative

Of course, you do not have time enough to address all of these great needs. So how can you know which ones to pursue? In part, this question is answered by the opportunities that open to you. In part, your own natural inclinations will guide you in recognizing which causes to pursue. And sometimes a line from your patriarchal blessing or a whispering from the Holy Ghost will guide you. But if you wait to move forward until you hear a voice from heaven telling you what to do, you may stand still for a very long time. Most often, finding which of your world's needs you can help meet is a combination of inspiration and your own God-given initiative.

The needs in your personal sphere of family, work, school, and friends are just as critical as the great needs of society.

University student Cara Marie Hadley used her own creativity and initiative to bring love to a difficult situation in her family's world:

"In July 2001, my only brother, Doug, was diagnosed with acute leukemia. Doug is one of my best friends, and I was devastated when I heard the news.

"That year, as Doug's birthday was approaching, I knew there was nothing I could do to help my 'hero-brother' medically. Still, I felt the need to do something to support and encourage him. I remembered reading about a group of Young Women who cut their hair and had it made into wigs for young cancer patients. Now I knew what I wanted to give my brother for his birthday—my hair. I would donate my hair in his name to a young girl with cancer so she would not have to suffer the indignity of being bald.

"For about two years I had been growing my hair out from a very short cut. I was about to start my freshman year at BYU–Idaho, and I was so excited that my hair was finally past my shoulders. But once the thought of cutting my hair entered my mind, I felt sure that I wanted to do it. On the Internet site locksoflove.com I found the information I needed. Each ponytail or braid had to be at least ten inches long. I was worried that my hair wouldn't be long enough. But a friend of mine who is a hair stylist braided my hair in three different braids— one in back and one on each side of my head. My sister cringed as she watched my friend slowly cut off each braid. One braid was 9¾ inches long, one was 10¼ inches, and one was 11 inches. I was so excited that my hair was really long enough!

"By the end of August, when I visited my brother in the hospital, he was totally bald. I handed him a sealed baggie with my braids inside. He looked up at me and then back at the baggie. When I told him I had cut my hair for him, he got tears in his eyes. I think he could feel the great love I have for him.

"A few days later, I mailed my hair to Florida, where it would be made into a wig and donated to a little girl who has lost her hair from cancer treatments. I like to think that some little girl feels happier because she doesn't have to go to school bald anymore."

mission moments

Your mission also extends to everyday matters. For example, you might notice that an acquaintance seems to be feeling unusually discouraged and blue. At that moment, you may be the only one on the scene to lend moral support, to take a minute to listen, to say words of appreciation and concern. Your decision to stop and help—to be a good Samaritan—may be the thing that turns your friend from some self-destructive decision or behavior. In that moment, you are doing something God needs *you* to do. In that tiny moment, you are fulfilling your mission.

A day is made up of many such moments. And each time you use your gifts to do something that God needs you to do—however large or small—you are fulfilling your mission. By praying for guidance and listening to the whisperings of the Holy Ghost, you can learn to recognize and respond to many such small needs in the course of your daily life—at home, at school, at work.

What are some of the everyday needs that you encounter in your world? What are some of the ways you can address them?

Truly, you are on a personal mission every day, and learning to perceive and fulfill that mission *now* can give you purpose, direction, and joy—even while the details of your future remain unknown at this point in your life.

To every [woman] there comes . . . that special
moment when [she] is figuratively tapped on the shoulder and
offered the chance to do a special thing unique to [her] and
fitted to [her] talent. What a tragedy if that moment finds [her]
unprepared for the work which would be [her] finest hour.
—Winston Churchill (as quoted in "'Sanctify Yourselves,'" 40)

Lighting the Way

HE DID NOT WANT ME TO FAIL

ERIKA THEW

In December 1997, when I returned from my mission to my home in Washington state, my future did not seem all that clear. A serious relationship that I had felt might lead to marriage did not seem to be working out, and I didn't seem to be receiving clear answers to my prayers. When the relationship ended, I felt that a rug had been pulled out from under me. But when I received an acceptance letter from the University of Utah, I saw a glimmer of hope, a path into the future.

Arriving at the university as a newly returned missionary in the habit of serving, I bounced around trying to find a student group that would fill my desire to serve. I also offered many prayers on the matter: "Where and what do you need me to be doing, Lord? How can I make a difference here?"

Every day when I picked up a copy of the university's student newspaper on campus, I noticed that its editorials and cartoons often shed a negative light on the Church's beliefs and practices. This was surprising to me because in every place I had lived before I had always respected the beliefs of others and felt that they respected mine. Now, frustrated by the way the Church and its members were being portrayed, I felt a need to stand up for our beliefs. I discussed the problem with the paper's editor and publisher but felt I was getting nowhere.

Feeling a bit helpless, I wondered how Latter-day Saint

Latter-day Saint views in an intelligent, scholarly, and professional way. Even the campus newspaper that was once so negative about the Church expressed respect for our publication and seems to have become more positive about the Church in general. *The Century* is now thriving in its second year.

Through this whole experience, the Lord never let us down. Although I was inexperienced and underqualified for this assignment, the Lord only required a willing heart and mind. He would not let me fail.

ERICA THEW IS STUDYING MASS COMMUNICATIONS AT THE UNIVERSITY OF UTAH. SHE ALSO WORKS PART TIME WITH THE TEEN MOTHER AND CHILD PROGRAM AT THE UNIVERSITY HOSPITAL AND TEACHES A FAMILY HISTORY CLASS IN HER WARD. ERICA ENJOYS TRAIL BIKING, RUNNING, DRAWING, AND PAINTING, AND IS LEARNING HOW TO KAYAK. SHE PLANS TO RETURN TO HER HOME STATE OF WASHINGTON AFTER GRADUATION.

Behold, the Lord requireth the heart and a willing mind.

—Doctrine and Covenants 64:34

chapter 5

YOUR OWN PATH

I believe I am always divinely guided.

I believe I will always take the right road.

I believe God will always make a way where there is no way.

—Anonymous

This stretch of your life's path holds many cross-roads—places where you will make decisions that will affect the rest of your life. It's natural to approach these with some uncertainty. After all, you've never been here before, and you can't know for sure what lies down the road in either direction. There may even be some unexpected detours. The good news is that many of the decisions you face offer you a lot of room to exercise your agency and to learn about personal revelation. Here are some thoughts to consider when you are standing at these crossroads, pondering your next step.

Education: To Survive and to Serve

It's wise to get the best education you can while you can. The more education you can obtain now, the more opportunities you will have later to make a contribution to your family, your community, and your world, and to support yourself and those you love. In other words, your education will help you serve *and* survive. A good education will also develop the gifts and talents the Lord has given you, resulting in personal growth and progression toward godliness. President Gordon B. Hinckley affirmed, "The Lord wants you to educate your minds and hands, whatever your chosen field. . . . Seek for the best schooling available. . . . You will bring honor to the Church and you will be generously blessed because of that training" ("A Prophet's Counsel and Prayer for Youth," *Ensign,* January 2001, 7).

Assess your talents, aptitudes, and interests. Be sure you pursue some post-high school program of training that will provide you with a marketable skill or will open up a field of career opportunities when it is completed. A four-year college degree is not for everyone, but you will be wise to set your sights on the highest level of training you can obtain. Education for its own sake is a wonderful thing, and so is being able to earn income. Plan for both. If you are pointed toward a college major such as sociology or communications, why not minor in a technology area or fulfill a secondary teaching certificate as well? This will maximize your earning potential throughout your life, offer more flexibility in your working schedule, and maximize your contribution to the world when you work. If your goal is to be a full-time mother when you have children at home, you will likely still have twenty other years in which you will work in paid employment and/or serve in voluntary positions outside the home. Obtaining productive skills now will benefit you in these various roles in the future, as well as helping you in your work as a homemaker and mother.

You don't need to go to a prestigious school to get a good education. You can often spend your education dollars more wisely by taking undergraduate courses at a community college or even on-line. Then, if you want to go to graduate school, you can choose a more specialized program at a more expensive university.

When you shop for colleges, look for LDS institute classes, student wards, and other programs the Church may have to offer to LDS students in the area. A student ward and/or institute program can make a great difference in your college experience, especially if you move away from home to go to school. In these settings you will find men and women your age who share your values and your commitment to the Savior, and who know how to have fun without the alcohol, drugs, or other immoral activities so common on college campuses today. You can also participate in service and social activities that will magnify your talents and give you valuable leadership experience.

Consider the moral environment of the college. Does it have a deserved reputation as a "party school"? Are dormitories coeducational, or are men and women housed separately?

As you make these decisions a matter of prayer and counsel with those who love you, the Lord will help you find educational opportunities that will equip you well to fulfill your personal mission over your lifetime.

what about a full-time mission?

Another crossroads that many young women encounter is whether to serve a full-time mission for the Church. The Lord and his church expect every able young Latter-day Saint man to serve a full-time mission. For young adult women, it is optional. It's a wonderful way to serve God and make an important contribution to spreading the gospel.

Your personal mission may or may not include a full-time mission. As a woman, you bring special gifts and talents to missionary work that are needed and valued. In every mission in the Church, sister missionaries fill important roles that elders cannot or do not fill as well. Some sister missionaries have special opportunities, such as serving at temple visitors centers or filling compassionate or humanitarian service assignments. And a full-time mission can offer spiritual learning and growth like few other experiences.

This crossroads truly is a marvelous opportunity to receive personal revelation and seek the Lord's will for your life. Seeking to maximize your contribution to God's work, both now and in the future, can be a helpful framework for making these decisions. If you do serve a full-time mission at this phase of your journey, you will be about the business of changing lives—others' as well as your own. If not, your personal growth and contributions can come in other ways equally significant and tailored for your life's path.

Dealing with Detours

Your own path is as personal as your fingerprints—unlike any other. And your personal mission can be found at every point along the way—whether your path follows a carefully planned course or takes a dramatic turn into the unexpected. Do you remember when a tornado picked up Dorothy Gale from her predictable life on a Kansas farm and dropped her off in totally unknown, and quite dangerous, territory? Looking down at her little dog, her only remaining connection to her familiar life, Dorothy observed, "Toto, I don't think we're in Kansas anymore." But it was in Oz, not Kansas, that Dorothy gained the gifts of wisdom and true friendship. What looked like a detour was actually an important part of her journey.

Most of us will face moments when our path doesn't lead where we thought it would, and we wonder whether our life hasn't somehow gone off course. Maybe you weren't able to go to the college you had always thought you'd attend. Or the opportunity to serve a full-time mission now seems exciting, although you had never planned to serve. Maybe you'll marry later than you thought, or not at all. Or maybe you'll marry sooner than you'd envisioned and want to put other plans on hold. Maybe you'll have more children than you planned, or fewer, or none. Even illness, injury, divorce, or death could at some point leave the landscape of your life looking unfamiliar.

But these kinds of detours are not at all unusual. Think of the young Hebrew boy Joseph who was sold into Egypt by his jealous brothers. It must have all seemed like a horrible circumstance. But the jarring detour from favored son in his father's house to stranger in a strange land actually enabled Joseph to save his whole family. Think of the infant Moses floating down the river in a basket—away from his mother and to a new life as Pharaoh's adopted son. Where did that detour lead? Or the women who packed up their belongings and walked across the frozen Mississippi River from Nauvoo and later civilized the Utah desert. Indeed, many of the people we see as heroes and heroines are people whose lives didn't follow the "normal" path. For all these people, special challenges were the wellspring from which their most important contributions were born.

The Real You: forming a positive personal identity

When someone asks you to tell something about yourself, what do you say first? You might tell about your job or schooling and whether you are married or single. If you were married, you would probably tell how many children you had. But while marital, family, and employment status are all convenient handles on which we can hang our identity, basing our sense of who we are on these labels alone can be problematic. School, job, and family status—all these are subject to change. And if we base our feelings of identity and worth solely on them, we can be shaken when our circumstances change. For example, if we base our feelings of worth primarily on our career achievements, we can find the transition to marriage and motherhood difficult. Or if we think that only marriage or students could have a positive voice on campus. How could those not of our faith receive a more accurate impression of our beliefs and views?

Several months later, my prayer to be of service was answered when I was assigned as publications chair on the Latter-day Saints Student Association council. My specific assignment was to develop an LDS student publication—to be distributed not only at the institute, but all over campus! I was ecstatic that the Lord was aware of the need and that I was going to be allowed to help.

When the work of putting together the new publication began, I felt overwhelmed. After all, at the time I was a psychology major, not a journalism major, and I had no editorial experience. Also, I was fairly new to the university. How could I produce a publication that would be both spiritual and professional in just a few months' time? Then, as I prayed, the realization came that I had nothing to fear. This wasn't my work alone, but the Lord's. He did not want me to fail, and he would be with me always.

Over the weeks that followed, the Lord sent person after person to help this work be accomplished. I called one young man to ask for his help with graphic design, another area about which I knew absolutely nothing. He said that he, too, had been looking for some way to serve and agreed to design our publication. Then the managing editor of the *Ensign* magazine arranged for me to meet with his staff, who gave me very valuable advice and guidance. Within a matter of months, our new publication, *The Century*, was born.

One of my favorite articles was an interview with Elder Cecil O. Samuelson of the Seventy, former dean of the University of Utah medical school. Our goal was to present motherhood will give us value, we will be vulnerable if those circumstances do not occur as we expect.

For women, ironically, marital status can be a stumbling block to a positive sense of self. A woman who marries later, or never marries, may feel this is the primary way she is identified. She may struggle with negative identifiers such as, "No one wants me," "I don't fit in a 'married' church," "I can't fulfill my purpose in life," or "This isn't the way I thought it would be." A woman who becomes divorced may add to these negatives a mistaken sense of personal failure or unworthiness. But women who are married struggle with issues of identity and worth as well. Women who are married often struggle to find a sense of individual identity because they sometimes feel overshadowed by their husbands' professional or church position or judged by their children's achievements. Or if their marriage or family is not perfect, they can have a sense of failure, inadequacy, or unworthiness, too. Yet each of these women has gifts and opportunities, some unique to her and some in common as women.

For example, a woman who has not married is able to immerse herself in a worthwhile career and make a contribution in that sphere—an option that is often out of the reach of a married woman with children. She may also have more freedom to travel, to pursue educational attainment, and to be involved in humanitarian organizations, community affairs, or worthwhile political causes. And she can have an impact as an aunt or a neighbor that is sometimes beyond the capacity of a busy mother. These are not small things, but they are not available to a woman who sees her singleness as a prime limiting fact of her identity.

the rock

A Primary song reminds us of a simple truth that the Savior taught:

> *The wise man built his house upon the rock,*
> *And the rains came tumbling down.*
> *The rains came down, and the floods came up, . . .*
> *And the house on the rock stood still.*
>
> *The foolish man built his house upon the sand,*
> *And the rains came tumbling down.*
> *The rains came down, and the floods came up, . . .*
> *And the house on the sand washed away.*
>
> (*Children's Songbook*, 281.)

So what is the "rock" upon which you can safely build your sense of personal identity and purpose? What are the core elements of your being, the things about you that don't change with circumstance? Consider the following:

1. You are a daughter of Heavenly Parents. Therefore, you have divine capabilities and endless potential to do good and experience joy.

2. You possess the fundamental gifts and endowments of womanhood, as well as your own individual gifts. These include the gifts of mothering, nurturing, and civilizing. You can use these gifts in every setting and circumstance throughout your life.

3. You have your own personal mission, which transcends your marital status and family circumstances. In whatever circumstance you find yourself, there is something special that you can contribute, something that perhaps only you can give.

You can learn to build your sense of self not on the shifting sand of personal circumstance, but on the rock of your eternal identity as a daughter of God, committed to fulfilling his individual plan for you.

Be thou humble; and the Lord thy God shall lead thee
by the hand, and give thee answer to thy prayers.
—Doctrine and Covenants 112:10

A Journey I Could Not Foresee

Camille Fronk

At age sixteen I received my patriarchal blessing. Unquestionably, the phrase that excited me most was one indicating that the Lord had blessed me with talents, only a few of which had been developed. For me, the promise of greater things to come was extremely motivating. I immediately began imagining various musical abilities that would miraculously become manifest in me. These were talents I saw as exciting; and they would also fit nicely into my picture of my future life as a wife and mother.

In the years that followed, that one line in my blessing—and the continued absence of musical gifts—prompted me to search for a broader understanding of talents from God and how to develop them. I found that Joseph Smith saw gifts and talents beyond the highly visible ones. He taught, "The greatest, the best, the most useful gifts would be known nothing about by an observer" (*Teachings of the Prophet Joseph Smith*, 246). I began to consider less obvious talents, such as listening to the Spirit, consideration for others, and the ability to graciously accept as well as give.

After college, my life began to move in a direction that was different from the one I had always envisioned. As I turned twenty-one, my bishop invited me to visit him in his office, where he issued an invitation to serve a mission. I had never yearned to serve a mission, thinking that at its completion I would be twenty-two and a half years old, which was frightfully old to not yet be married. But my bishop said he felt strongly that the Lord wanted me to go. When I shared this news with my father, his reaction was that the Lord did not require his daughters to go on missions. What was I to do? Pulled between these contradictory views, I knew I needed to find out for myself. I went to my knees and poured out my heart to God as I had never done before. I expected an answer by the time I stood up, but nothing came. Weeks went by. I tried fasting—serious fasting. Still no answer. Or so I thought. Then finally I began to perceive a quiet answer, a subtle feeling I had had all along. I realized the Spirit had been telling me what God wanted me to do—I simply hadn't known what to look for.

For me the answer was yes, go on a mission. With some anxiety, I accepted a call to serve eighteen months in Toulouse, France. There, while focused on communicating truths that meant everything to me, in a language that was foreign to me, I somehow lost my shyness and discovered a love for teaching scripture and doctrine. When I returned home, to my surprise I was invited to teach seminary, at a time when women serving as full-time seminary teachers were virtually nonexistent.

While teaching seminary, I also began pursuing a graduate degree in Near Eastern Studies, feeding my long-standing interest in the ancient world. During my last semester, while studying in Jerusalem, I became discouraged. Certainly, this was not the life I had pictured as a Mormon girl growing up in Tremonton, Utah. At this crucial time, I discovered a line in my patriarchal blessing that made a connection between developing talents and gaining greater knowledge. I also discovered a corresponding passage in the Doctrine and Covenants, where the Lord promised his enabling power when we seek after knowledge (see D&C 88:80). From these discoveries, I knew that God's commands would be my "enablings." As a result, I came to see completing my graduate degree as a way to prepare to better serve God how, where, and whenever he might call.

This new focus formed a foundation for many decisions and opportunities that followed. I was invited to serve as dean of students at LDS Business College, then to be the first woman to teach full time at the LDS Institute of Religion adjacent to the University of Utah, and finally to earn a Ph.D. degree in sociology of the Middle East and join the Ancient Scripture faculty at BYU. As I pursued these unforeseen paths, I began to experience a power and facility to learn, to see connections, and to teach scripture that I had never known before. Abilities beyond my natural capacity started to emerge.

A spiritual sense of direction and growth did not, however, prevent me from encountering opposition. My life's path, though very exciting and challenging, was oftentimes unsettling because it increasingly diverged from my childhood dreams about adulthood. As I passed through my twenties and thirties, marriage and family appeared increasingly elusive. My academic career was in an area not traditionally pursued by women and required increased commitment. During this time, many well-meaning people tried to discourage me from pursuing the course my life was taking, arguing that I was limiting my chances for marriage. But I had felt the gentle encouragement from the Spirit and experienced success in ways that I knew had nothing directly to do with me. In short, I was learning to be led by the Spirit, and the results were miraculous to me.

I still do not know where this journey will lead. I haven't

figured out why the Lord has encouraged me down a less-traveled path. What would have seemed impossible to me at sixteen years of age has now become a remarkable blessing. My opportunities to serve include a full-time career teaching religion to young adults, doing research among Palestinians in the West Bank and Gaza Strip, and taking part in humanitarian expeditions to Third World countries. I now gladly accept the direction of my life and give God thanks. Challenges will always come and mirages of dead ends will occasionally appear, but when you follow the mission to which the Lord has called you, it will always be right.

CAMILLE FRONK IS AN ASSISTANT PROFESSOR OF ANCIENT SCRIPTURE AT BRIGHAM YOUNG UNIVERSITY AND SERVES AS A PRIMARY TEACHER IN HER WARD. SHE ENJOYS NATURE, OUTDOOR ACTIVITIES, AND SPENDING TIME WITH HER IMMEDIATE FAMILY AND HER MANY NIECES AND NEPHEWS IN UTAH.

Trust in the Lord with all thine heart;
and lean not unto thine own understanding.
In all thy ways acknowledge him,
and he shall direct thy paths.

—Proverbs 3:5–6

section II

CHALLENGES ALONG
YOUR WAY

chapter 6

MEETING THE MORAL
CHALLENGES
OF YOUR WORLD

We will "stand as witnesses of God at all times
and in all things and in all places."
—Young Women Theme

The years after high school bring a new phase of life—a larger world, with perhaps a new school or job experience. During this phase, you may move away from your parents' house or even leave your hometown altogether. Maybe for the first time in your life you can come and go as you please—with no questions asked by concerned parents.

Of course, in your post-Young Women years, "personal progress" is strictly up to you. There will be no medallion to symbolize your success in reaching your spiritual goals. In fact, the larger world outside your home and Church may actively punish the very values you worked hard to cultivate in the Young Women program. You may feel pressure to use the alcohol or drugs that sometimes flow freely at college or work parties. You may feel like a prude if you don't use some of the crude language you hear at school or at work or if you don't go to the latest R-rated movie that everyone is seeing. Your college professors may make light of your religious values. Some people will regard your commitment to postpone sexual activity until marriage as ridiculous.

You may have stood literally hundreds of times during your teenage years and pledged to "stand as [a witness] of God at all times and in all things, and in all places." And now you are experiencing just how challenging that can be. How can you stay true to your values when so many voices around you say that you are naïve, narrow-minded, or repressed?

First, remember you are not alone. More than a million young Latter-day Saint women worldwide share these challenges. And God has promised that, if we invite him, he will send divine, even miraculous, help: "For I will go before your face. I will be on your right hand and on your left, and my

Spirit shall be in your hearts, and mine angels round about you, to bear you up" (D&C 84:88).

How can you "stand as a witness" when the world calls for you to fall for its ways?

A polluted Moral Environment

The first step is simply to *see.* Many of us today live in cities where the air is smoggy and hazy most of the time. We may sometimes even forget what clean air looks like—how blue the sky is and how much closer and crystal-clear things appear when the air is clean—until a strong wind briefly blows the pollution away. Our cultural environment is polluted in a similar way. Often we do not even realize how polluted it is because we are so accustomed to it. But if we take a look back forty or fifty years, the contrast is startling.

For example, within your parents' lifetime—

•Profane or coarse language, including taking the Lord's name in vain, was not allowed on television. Neither were references to or depictions of sexual activity, either heterosexual or homosexual.

•References to bodily functions or "bathroom humor" were not found in public life.

•Popular music did not contain profanity or lyrics glorifying murder, rape, or suicide.

•Most mainstream adult movies would have been rated G or PG, instead of PG-13 or R. Nudity was not a standard part of adult movies; romantic episodes stopped short of the bedroom and did not include sexual content designed to be overtly arousing.

•Pornography was relegated to back rooms of magazine

and book stores—instead of being instantly available on a home computer screen at the click of a button.

•Violence in movies and television was not sensationalized. There was little gore and no prolonged or brutal beatings. Human brutality was not portrayed as exciting, and it was not interactive, as in today's video games, where children can decapitate or dismember someone on screen in bloody detail.

•Television talk shows were usually wholesome, instead of forums for unhappy people to parade their self-destructive choices before the world.

•People dressed modestly in public.

•Swearing and profanity were considered inappropriate in public and were not heard in school halls and office elevators.

Just as those who have lived only in a big city may accept smoggy air as normal, those who have come of age in the last ten years may not realize how low the standards of our civilization have fallen. But dirty air is always unhealthy to the human body, whether or not we see it; in extreme cases it even causes death. In a similar way, morally dirty media is unhealthy to the human body, mind, and spirit—and it can also lead to physical and spiritual death. And just as breathing in pure air brings health and strength to the body and all its organs, the intake of morally pure influences is essential to the spiritual health and strength of human beings, both individually and collectively.

In a world where entertainment plays such a significant role in life, how can you avoid being exposed to the spiritually toxic waste it dumps into your environment? You have probably found some ways to do this; here are a few more suggestions:

•Substitute other recreational activities for movies and television watching. With a group of friends, try bowling, archery, roller-blading, or sledding, or hold a regular game night. By yourself, you could visit an art gallery or a museum. Take a walk with headphones and uplifting music. Discover a new, morally positive author and start reading through his or her works.

•Assume that even PG-13 movies contain objectionable material and avoid them, unless you have specific information to the contrary. (You can check for negative movie and video content on the Internet at www.screenit.com. Warning: The descriptions of objectionable elements in movies can sometimes themselves be objectionable.)

•Instead of going out to a movie, invite friends over to watch old classic movies at home. There are so many in every category: mystery (*The Thin Man* series), comedy (*The Road to* series or anything with Cary Grant, Jerry Lewis, Bob Hope, or Bing Crosby), drama (*Anna Karenina*). Or pick an actor such as James Stewart or Katharine Hepburn and go through his or her repertoire.

•Get a good Internet filter to help you avoid all the clever ways pornographers have of putting their products on your screen.

Dressing for Respect

One of the best ways you can "stand as a witness of God" is in the way you dress. How do you want to be treated by those around you? With respect and dignity? How do you hope that young men—and eventually your husband—will treat you? Do you want them to see you as a person first, a soul who has feelings and thoughts? Do you want to help them keep their thoughts clean or be a stumbling block to them? The way you choose to dress plays a big role in determining how others—particularly men—perceive and treat you.

Men's sexual responses are more easily triggered by visual stimuli than are women's. Tight clothing that accentuates the shape of a woman's bust or bottom, clothing that is strapless, off-the-shoulder, low-cut, or shows cleavage, or bares her stomach, back, or thigh immediately draws a man's attention to that part of the woman's body. These visual cues usually trigger sexually oriented feelings, which the man may or may not choose to suppress. He will find it difficult *not* to think of the woman as a physical object first, rather than as a human soul.

If this is hard for you to believe, it is probably because this is not how *you* respond to visual stimuli. And, you might think, if you can control your thoughts, why shouldn't men be able to? Simply stated, men are "wired" differently than women. Their reaction is, at least in part, a matter of biology. So when you wear revealing clothing, you are creating a stumbling block for men around you. And this is something the Lord may hold us accountable for as women.

On the other hand, when you dress modestly, you help men think of you as a person first, not as an object of physical desire. This does not mean that you should strive to look unattractive, but rather *to be attractive in a modest way.* Many of the styles for young women today are immodest. Some are *very* immodest. But because standards have changed so much in the last ten years, you may not recognize it. So dressing modestly is a challenge. When you get dressed, take a hard look in the mirror and ask, "Does my clothing cling to my body and accentuate my bust and hips? Does my cleavage show, or can someone see down my shirt when I lean forward? Is more of my thigh showing than is not showing? Is my midriff showing?"

You might also ask, "Does my clothing call attention to my body or my beliefs?" Or to put it another way, "Am I wearing the uniform of a daughter of God or a singer on a music video?" You might also think about whether you would feel embarrassed if the prophet were to walk into the room and shake your hand. You can also ask for feedback from your mother, a female seminary or institute teacher, or an LDS friend. Above all, pray and ask your Heavenly Father how he wants you to look to others.

As you dress in a way that shows respect for yourself and your male friends, you will help to de-sexualize the atmosphere between women and men. This is good for both women and men. Today, more than ever, the Lord needs young Latter-day Saint women to "stand as a witness" by dressing modestly.

The path to true love

We've all heard someone (often a male) call a movie a "chick flick." It's a movie that usually makes men yawn and women sigh (or cry). This kind of movie usually has a romantic theme. That is, it shows the triumph of true love over some obstacle that has threatened the union of the hero and heroine.

Almost every woman wants to find "true love," a loving and lasting romantic relationship. True love is unselfish and noble. It is the kind of love the Lord intended for us when he created us male and female. A man who truly loves you would climb the highest mountain or walk over burning coals for you—or at least run to the store for you to get you chocolate or Tylenol. But how can women in today's world actually find that kind of love—love that doesn't seek to exploit them, but seeks to serve their best good? And what does sexual morality have to do with this quest?

Imagine you and a romantic partner are standing at a crossroads. In one direction lies "True Love," in the other "Selfish Love." Actually, the term "selfish love" is a contradiction in terms—sort of like "giant shrimp." Love that doesn't act for the ultimate well-being of the beloved is a fake.

Selfish Love or True Love?

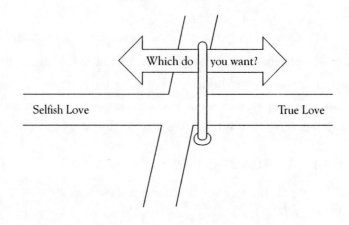

Imagine that each time you and your partner interact, you move in one direction or the other—and closer to one kind of love or the other. In particular, the physical part of your relationship will determine which direction you are heading.

The only sure way to find true and unselfish love, as opposed to selfish and exploitive love, is to live the law of chastity. This law requires that you abstain from any sexual contact outside of marriage. President Spencer W. Kimball taught that when physical passion is indulged outside of marriage, "pure love is pushed out one door while lust sneaks in the other" (*Faith Precedes the Miracle*, 154). Each time you violate the spirit of the law of chastity, you move toward selfish love, where each partner uses the other for personal gratification. Each time you honor this law, you move toward true love—regardless of whether that love eventually culminates in marriage or not.

The law of chastity is both a great protection and a great gift for women. It protects you from physical exploitation and emotional pain and suffering. It protects you from becoming emotionally bonded—and maybe even marrying—someone with whom you are not compatible. And it can lead you toward the deepest and truest kind of love—eternally "true" love.

To understand how the law of chastity does this, it is helpful to understand certain aspects of human nature.

Different needs. *Men and women have different needs and drives regarding physical intimacy.* Women generally have a stronger need for emotional bonding and closeness, and these feelings are easily triggered by romantic expressions from a man. Men typically have a stronger sex drive, which is nearer the surface and more easily triggered by visual stimuli or touch. For women, physical intimacy is typically an ultimate expression of love and sacrifice. For men, physical intimacy is not necessarily an ultimate expression of love. Rather, commitment and marriage are a man's ultimate expression of love and sacrifice.

A selfish act. *Physical intimacy outside of marriage is always a selfish act.* When a couple is physically intimate before marriage, they place their relationship on a selfish foundation, whether they intend to or not. President Spencer W. Kimball described it this way:

"Sexual encounters outside of legalized marriage *render the individual a thing to be used, a thing to be exploited,* and make him or her exchangeable, exploitable, expendable. . . . [This] destroys their being and loses for them their self. . . . We really do not '*love*' things. We *use* things like doormats, automobiles, clothing, machines; *but we love people by serving them and contributing to their permanent good*" (*Faith Precedes the Miracle,* 155–56; some italics added).

Strong bonds. *Physical intimacy creates strong emotional bonds that cannot be broken without emotional and spiritual damage to both partners.* When a man is physically intimate with a woman without making the ultimate commitment of marriage to her, he begins to view her as an object, the means of his physical gratification. This physical drive or bond is so strong that he may pursue it at the expense of her personal welfare. And the end of the relationship can cause him to have strong, destructive feelings of jealousy and anger. When a woman makes the ultimate sacrifice of physical intimacy without having obtained the ultimate sacrifice of marital commitment from her partner, she forms an emotional bond and a personal vulnerability is created. Having "cast [her] pearls before swine" (see Matthew 7:6), the foundation of her self-respect and inner strength is weakened. She becomes dependent on him for emotional validation and she may be committed to him even if he is not a good companion for her. The end of the relationship—the negating of her ultimate offering of self—can be emotionally and spiritually devastating to her.

Physical Consequences. In addition to these spiritually destructive effects, sexual immorality often causes physical destruction as well. Some sexually transmitted diseases cannot be prevented by contraceptive devices, and no type of contraception is 100 percent effective in preventing pregnancy.

Inevitable human error increases the fallibility of so-called safe-sex measures, causing the threat of HIV infection and pregnancy to be ever-present in sex outside of marriage.

Moving in the Right Direction

Some couples may think that they can move in the direction of selfish love—doing things that are progressively more passionate, but stopping just before they think they would need to confess to their bishop. While they may think they are keeping the letter of the law, this behavior moves their relationship farther and farther from true love, making their interactions more selfish and harmful to each other—which is, in itself, a sin. Some engaged couples may think, "It's all right to become more physically involved now. We've saved ourselves for each other, and we'll be married soon. What we're doing is just bringing us closer." Such a couple is not only jeopardizing the precious blessing of a temple sealing, but—by focusing on their own physical pleasure—they are already giving up the spiritual blessings it offers, since they have turned their relationship in the direction of selfish love and lust. Any interaction between an unmarried couple that is physically arousing moves them in the wrong direction on the path of love and is morally wrong.

One of the saddest aspects of sexual sin is that a woman who has sexual relations before marriage will never know if her partner loves who she is more than he wants her body, or if he loves her well-being more than he loves his own physical pleasure. The simple truth is this: After marriage, physical passion can be an expression and symbol of true, giving love. Before marriage, it destroys it.

If you have gone down the path of physical lust in your

romantic relationships, you need to change, and you can. This behavior is spiritually destructive to you and to your partner and is therefore very serious, even if it may be accepted among some of your Latter-day Saint peers. You can repent, and the Lord wants you to do so. If you have had physical contact that goes beyond kissing and hugging, you should go to your bishop and explain your situation, and ask for his help. The Lord does not love us *less* when we transgress, but we cannot "abide in his love" and have his Spirit to be with us unless we repent and live his laws (see John 15:10). As you confess, repent of, and forsake these behaviors, you can reclaim the purity and peace that living the law of chastity brings. It is not too late, and it will put you back on the path of fulfilling the personal mission God has for you.

Homosexuality: a gospel-based view

One of the great moral challenges today is the question of homosexuality. Even though only about three percent of men and two percent of women identify themselves as actively homosexual, homosexuality is portrayed in television and movies as a very common, and completely acceptable, alternative lifestyle. It is openly discussed on high school and college campuses; it is lobbied for in local, state, and national government.

The Church's teachings on the subject are clear. The marital union of man and woman is the basis of eternal family life. And *any* sexual relationship outside of this union is a sin. Still you may wonder: "Is homosexuality genetically determined, or is it a matter of choice? And how can it be wrong if it isn't a choice? Don't homosexual people have a right to be happy and accepted?"

Scientific evidence indicates that while biological and environmental factors can both play a role in influencing sexual orientation, so does choice. As with all difficult questions, the scriptures give us crucial perspectives. One of these is that "the natural man is an enemy to God" (see Mosiah 3:19). In other words, many of our "natural" inclinations and impulses can produce destructive results. Left on their own, most small children would eat only candy, which would be harmful to them. They need parents to guide them to eat foods that will make them healthy. Similarly, most anthropologists agree that males of our species are not biologically programmed to be monogamous. That is, left to their natural feelings, they would have many sexual partners. However, like the loving parent who teaches a child to eat healthy foods, Heavenly Father has lovingly given men and women laws of moral conduct to follow, not leaving them to experience the destruction that comes from following their natural impulses. One of these laws is a prohibition against homosexual behavior.

Sometimes young women who excel in areas traditionally identified as "masculine" and not in areas traditionally regarded as "feminine" begin to think that they are not fundamentally feminine. And some young women may feel alienated from stereotypes of "femininity" that they find shallow or demeaning or simply not in harmony with their own sense of self. Some young women may have had negative or hurtful experiences with men in their lives—either in family or peer relationships—which have caused them to feel alienated from romantic desires toward men. Any of these experiences may cause a young woman to wonder about her sexual identity. But this does not mean that she is abnormal or homosexual. At the same time, she should be very careful to avoid any kind of experimentation in this area. Contrary to how it might seem, homosexual relationships cannot provide a happy solution to these challenges.

For each young woman—no matter what her personality or experiences—God has a plan to bring her true happiness. Part of this plan is for her to learn to develop Christlike relationships with men—in marriage, if possible, and in brotherly/sisterly associations in families, in the Church, and in society. The many differences between men and women—while sometimes puzzling and challenging—bring growth for both men and women as they work together in these associations. Through loving and serving each other, both men and women become more godly—which is, after all, the fundamental purpose of our earthly life.

We all know someone—perhaps even someone close to us—who identifies herself or himself as homosexual. In the words of President Gordon B. Hinckley, "Our hearts reach out to those who struggle with feelings of affinity for the same gender. We remember you before the Lord, we sympathize with you, we regard you as our brothers and our sisters. However, we cannot condone immoral practices on your part any more than we can condone immoral practices on the part of others" ("Stand Strong," *Ensign*, November 1995, 99). At the same time, we must be sure to treat people in this situation as Christ would have us do, not with ridicule or condemnation but with concern and compassion.

Why has the Lord defined homosexual behavior as a serious sin? Sins are behaviors and attitudes that are destructive to ourselves and others. They cannot lead us back to God; in fact, they lead us away from him. They make us miserable, and ultimately they destroy us. Homosexuality is a way of life that cannot produce true and lasting happiness for anyone involved. On the contrary, it leads to frustration, self-absorption, sexual excess, and despair. On a societal level, homosexuality is destructive as well. It prevents the formation of families, the birth of children, and their rearing in a wholesome environment. Historically, the rise of homosexual practices has signaled and caused the decline of civilizations.

Turning the Tide

As a young adult woman in this modern world, you stand in a paradoxical position. On the one hand, you have been selected by Satan as the main target and victim of one of his most destructive campaigns—the sexualization and coarsening of all aspects of society, the glamorization of provocative and suggestive clothing, and the total acceptance and normalization of sex outside of marriage and of pornography and homosexuality. All of these things hurt women more directly than they do men. Why is this so? Perhaps it is as Sister Patricia Holland has suggested, "If I were Satan and wanted to destroy a society, I think I would stage a full-blown blitz on its women" (A Quiet Heart, 43). And yet, paradoxically, you have been endowed with innate female strengths that especially enable you to resist these attacks and turn the tide of the battle. Like Queen Esther, you have been prepared to save your people and your civilization.

If this sounds too burdensome and not very fun, we hope you will remember this: God's plan for his daughters and sons has been called "the great plan of happiness." He sent his Son into the world that we might "have life, and that [we] might have it more abundantly" (John 10:10). If you will respond to these tremendous moral challenges by steadfastly following

what Elder Boyd K. Packer has referred to as the Lord's "rules
of happiness" ("The Father and the Family," 20), two things
will happen. Not only will you fulfill the crucial part the Lord
needs you to play in this great struggle; you will also find
that—just as he promised us—your joy can truly be full (see
John 15:11).

And there [was not] . . . any manner of lasciviousness;
and surely there could not be a happier people among all the people
who had been created by the hand of God.

—4 Nephi 1:16

Lighting the way

In Good Company

Lisa Ann Jackson

Trinity Dam is a blue-green lake nestled in the mountains of Northern California. The dense forest comes right up to the red-clay beaches and sun-drenched docks. For the last several years, this has been the setting of an annual outing for a group of LDS young single adults from the San Francisco Bay area. It's a fun weekend packed with camping, water-skiing, wake-boarding, swimming, kayaking, and plenty of eating. And it takes place over Labor Day weekend, which usually includes a fast Sunday.

The first year I attended, I didn't know many people on the trip. I wasn't sure how they would handle certain situations (sleeping arrangements, Sunday activities, and fasting), nor how I might handle them in their company. Then I saw the schedule for the weekend and realized that my worries were unnecessary. The organizers matter-of-factly stated the itinerary: arrival and skiing on Friday, skiing on Saturday, church and free time on Sunday, skiing and departure on Monday. The meal schedule was also given: big breakfasts, big dinners, and sandwiches in between, no breakfast on Sunday morning, and a big lunch on Sunday afternoon.

Many things happened over the weekend to demonstrate to me that these were good people. But when they made it so easy for me to keep the Sabbath and to fast, I knew I was in company of people I could call friends.

During the years after leaving my family and before start-
ing one of my own, my friends have become my surrogate
family. They are the people with whom I spend much of my
time. They are the people who have influenced my choices as
I have established my identity and habits that will go with me
into my own family. And ultimately one of my male friends
will become the one with whom I will establish that family.
This has been a crucial time to seek out friends who, by their
actions and influence, make it easier for me to live the gospel.

The year I returned home from my mission, my first companion in the mission field invited me to live with her. She
had selected a group of girls to live with and found an apartment for us. All of us had served missions, and all of us now
faced the transition back into what seemed like the selfish
schedule of school and social life. This was a time when I was
deciding for myself if I would read the scriptures each day, what
activities I would do or not do on Sundays, how I would filter
movies and other media, and how I would serve in my callings.
Without parents in my home or a white handbook in my
pocket, I was left to choose how valiant I would be. That
school year, each roommate silently set an example for me of
how to keep the good habits formed in their upbringing and
missions—daily prayer, scripture study, service, and hard work.
These women did not leave me as they found me. They
inspired me. It was easy to live the gospel in this home.

My roommates during college were all members of the
Church, but not all of those I call friends are necessarily members. I have many good associates who may not share all my
values or beliefs, but they do understand them, respect them,
and help me honor them. True friends never ask me to be less
than I should be and consistently help me be more than I am.

Of course, my ultimate friend is the Savior, Jesus Christ, who sets the perfect example of a true friend. He has charity and long-suffering for my shortcomings. He offers gentle, and sometimes strong, nudgings to follow him. He is patient and kind, but firm in his commands. He wants the best for me, and he helps me achieve my highest potential. He is also unwavering. There have been and will continue to be times that, despite my best efforts, I have struggled to find close associates who share or respect my desires to live the gospel. I have been in circumstances where there simply were few people who shared my values or interests. I have also had efforts to develop friendships rejected. Throughout these times the Savior has stood steadfast with me as I have stood steadfast with him.

In my life, I have found that, as I cling to the Savior and my Heavenly Father and cultivate the company of people striving to live their best, my path is made much easier. For me, the friendship of good people has been a blessed gift amid the thorns of mortality.

HAVING MOVED THIRTY-EIGHT TIMES IN HER LESS-THAN-THIRTY-EIGHT YEARS, LISA ANN JACKSON HAS OFTEN BEEN IN THE POSITION OF MAKING NEW FRIENDS. SHE HAS LIVED IN CALIFORNIA, NEVADA, UTAH, COLORADO, ENGLAND, AND GERMANY, BUT SHE CLAIMS COLORADO AS HOME. SHE CURRENTLY LIVES IN UTAH, WHERE SHE IS AN EDITOR FOR THE *LIAHONA*, THE CHURCH'S INTERNATIONAL MAGAZINE. LISA ALSO ENJOYS MOUNTAIN BIKING, WATER SKIING, SINGING, AND THE ARTS.

Choose your friends carefully.

It is they who will lead you in one direction or the other.

—Gordon B. Hinckley ("A Prophet's Counsel and Prayer,"
Ensign, January 2001, 7)

chapter 7

LOOKING FOR TRUE LOVE:
DATING AND MARRIAGE DECISIONS

That [your] hearts might be comforted, being knit together in love.
—Colossians 2:2

I nstitute classes, multi-stake dances, firesides, singles wards, hanging out with friends, school, work, parties, even shopping . . . With so many ways to meet people, why do good men sometimes seem so hard to find? Do you ever worry that you will never find that "needle in a haystack" you are searching for—that person who seems truly right for you— especially when so much of the dating process is out of your control?

It may be reassuring for you to know that, statistically, the large majority of Latter-day Saint women do marry and that the large majority of those have children. In other words, even though you may not be dating much (or even at all) right now, it is likely you will eventually marry. So let's talk about some very important questions:

- What are you looking for in a husband?
- How can you meet and get to know that kind of young man?
- How can you know when you have found a good marriage partner?

Although it might seem so at times, it is not all that difficult to meet handsome, exciting, fun young men. *The trick is to find a young man who is some of those things* and *a good potential marriage partner.* It is simply true that no matter how handsome and fun a young man is, if he does not have good moral character, he will make you unhappy in marriage. Likewise, statistically speaking, marrying someone who does not share your religious commitment puts you at a very high risk for divorce or for falling away from church commitment yourself.

So how can you improve your chances of meeting and marrying the kind of person with whom you can have an eternal marriage? There are no foolproof formulas, but here are some strategies that have been helpful to others.

1. Be actively engaged in a good cause. Go about your life, fulfilling your personal mission, doing good, growing, having fun, and being happy. Rather than waiting to start your life until you have met someone who will give it meaning, go about the business of *creating* meaning and purpose in your life. Then, if you don't find Mr. Right, you'll be happy anyway. If you do meet a likely candidate for marriage, you will be in the most positive and attractive frame of mind for a relationship to blossom.

2. Work at being the kind of person you would like to live with for the rest of your life. Simply stated, you will tend to attract the quality of person that you are. If you have self-respect, you will tend to attract someone who will respect you. The way you take care of your physical appearance is one outward signal of the way you value and respect yourself, as is the way you dress. And taking some time to assess the inner you and working to make significant improvements will help you attract a better quality person to spend your life with.

3. Be friendly, not forward; let him seek after you. Even though social norms have changed and it is considered acceptable for women to ask men for a date, human nature has not changed. Generally, it is still to your advantage to let men do most of the asking, arranging, and paying for dates. There are exceptions to this, but generally it is better that the man make more of the effort and sacrifice in the courtship process. This arrangement sets a pattern for the man to take care of you and sacrifice for you. It is also generally more appealing to men to be the ones initiating and pursuing, rather than being the one pursued. And besides, if he doesn't value you enough to make a little effort, you probably don't want him.

4. Instead of just dating, have as your goal "getting to know the other person." It helps to spend time doing a wide variety of activities beyond the traditional dinner and a movie or a dance. Seeing him interact with his family and inviting him to an activity with yours can be enlightening as well.

5. Set limits for your own physical and emotional involvement. Set physical limits. Remember, there is a fine line between expressing affection and expressing lust. The line is crossed whenever sexual feelings are aroused. Affection strengthens the relationship; lust places one or both of the partners in a position of being used as an object for the other's satisfaction. It changes the focus of the relationship from the mutual good of each partner to one's own physical pleasure and sets the relationship on a destructive foundation. It creates strong bonds between the partners—bonds that could cause incompatible partners to marry. Before going on a date, be clear about the boundaries over which you will not cross.

Consider this idea: *Save your kisses for someone and something special.* Dating and kissing do not have to go together, and you are not obligated to kiss someone after going out with him a certain number of times. Why not wait to kiss until the relationship has progressed to the point that a kiss can mean "You are special; I am interested in you more than any other"? And then just give a goodnight kiss until you are engaged. Kissing fans the flames of emotional involvement for women and leaves both individuals wanting more physically.

Here are twelve simple rules that will help you keep your dating relationships on a foundation of unselfishness, with the potential to grow into real love. They will help you keep your dates focused on the non-physical aspects of getting to know each other. They will help you keep in place boundaries for what is appropriate. Some of them will seem outdated, compared to the world's standards. Just remember: The world does not care whether or not you find true love. The Lord does.

- Don't enter a house or bedroom alone with a man.
- Don't recline or lie down beside a man.
- Don't park in a secluded place with your date.
- Don't participate in open-mouthed, passionate, or prolonged kissing.
- Don't touch each other's body in any way that is sexually arousing; don't handle each other's bodies anywhere that would be covered by temple garments, either under or on top of clothing.
- Don't remove any clothing.
- Don't take co-ed overnight or camping trips without married adult chaperones and separate sleeping accommodations.
- Do plan dates where you do fun activities, preferably with others, rather than sitting around alone together.
- Do spend time with and get to know each other's families.
- Do set a reasonable curfew ahead of time and stick to it. No all-night dates.
- Do date members of the Church who have high moral standards.
- Do pray about your date, before and after.

You can also adopt other personal rules that can help keep you on the path of true love and personal purity.

Set emotional limits. When a woman is too eager to "fall in love," it places her in a position of weakness or vulnerability. It is better for you, and for the relationship, if you hold back a little and do not get very emotionally invested in the relationship until he has given you some indication that he is seriously interested.

6. Being in love is important—but it is not enough. A common theme of many romantic movies and television shows is that the only necessary ingredient for a happy relationship is that both people be passionately in love with each other.

Romantic passion is surely one of the most wonderful gifts the Lord has given us. Yet for all of the importance we place on it, it is interesting that nowhere in the scriptures are we commanded to "be in love." Instead, we are commanded to love others, unselfishly and unceasingly. Perhaps this is because the Lord knows that feelings of romantic love vanish without loving behavior to sustain and magnify them.

For many women, falling in love is not that difficult to do; the challenge is to fall in love with someone with whom you can have a mutually loving relationship. Here are some questions to help you tell whether you have found someone with whom you can be eternally happy:

- Is he committed to the gospel?
- Does he have good character?
- Does he meet his obligations and keep his commitments?
- Can he be counted on?
- Is he trustworthy and honest?
- Does he make you want to be and do your best (and vice versa)?
- Is he unselfish?
- Is he responsible with money?

• Is he a good problem solver?

• Is he kind and considerate with you and with others?

• Are you comfortable with his family and the way he treats them?

You are not looking for Mr. Perfect, but your mate does need to have some of these positive qualities in order to make a happy marriage possible. This is important because being in an unhappy marriage is worse than being single. Remember that your partner will not change much after the wedding, and, more important, *you will not change him.* So now is the time to choose the qualities that will maximize your chances of having a lasting, joyful marriage. And you can do this by choosing a compatible person of good character. If you fall in love with someone with whom you can't be happy, you need to let go and move on, both for your happiness and that of your future children.

7. Be willing to accept the Lord's timetable for you and to make the most of your single years. Most women will marry at some time in their lives. We also know that even those who do not marry in this life will have the opportunity to marry and rear children in the next life. But these facts can seem like cold comfort at times of loneliness and yearning. And the fact that the Church's social structure and theology are built around families can contribute to feelings of being left out and discounted as a single person. But the Lord sees every one of his daughters—whether single or married—as a whole and valuable person. And he has important contributions for each one to make and a mission for each to fulfill. A single life brings opportunities that are different from those of married women with children. By focusing on magnifying our talents and gifts and using them to contribute to God's work, we can rise above frustrations and dissatisfaction with circumstances that we cannot fully control, and find joy and fulfillment at every stage of life.

Ready or Not

Maybe you have been to a wedding shower where the married women offer advice to the bride-to-be. This is done because getting ready for marriage is a little like packing for a trip to the moon: unless you have a clear picture of what it's going to be like, it's hard to prepare. Unfortunately, most of us approach marriage with more myths than realities in our minds, and by the time the shower takes place, it's a little late to get ready. What are some of these myths, and how can you prepare for marriage more realistically?

"If I find the 'right' one, marriage will be a happily-ever-after existence with few problems and difficulties." While most of us rationally know that this is not true, our hearts are still influenced by the fairy tale idea of marriage. Somehow we hope, and even expect, that married life will be an idyllic state of existence that will make us gloriously happy. Then, when we begin to experience problems, complexities, and challenges, we wonder if something is wrong with our marriage— or with our marriage partner. But the reality is that married life is still *life*. And challenges and problems are normal in life, whether married or single. Married life also presents the additional soul-stretching challenge of working out a healthy relationship with a husband. Sometimes, when problems arise, the woman may feel that her husband is wrecking her "perfect" marriage. But marriage is a place where people work out problems together, and learning to do this can be enormously satisfying.

"Since I'll be living with my best friend, I'll never feel lonely again." Although you may consider your husband to be your best friend, his friendship will probably be different from your girl friendships. Women and men are quite different, so your husband will not be likely to think or react exactly as you or your girlfriends do. Achieving emotional intimacy with you may not be as high a priority for him. He may not need to, or even want to, talk much about his feelings. And when you talk about yours, he may respond in different ways than you expect—offering solutions, for example, rather than listening and empathizing. But that will not mean that he doesn't love you.

Having complementary traits—with one partner being more rational and one more emotional, for example—can actually be a positive aspect of husband-wife relationships. Marriages and families benefit from having individuals with complementary or even opposite strengths. It's sort of like being able to play both the white keys *and* the black keys of the piano. You *can* make music with just one set or the other, but with both sets your music can be even richer. So rather than seeing differences as negative and frustrating, you'll need to appreciate your husband's strengths, especially those that are different from yours.

"If I ever stop feeling 'in love,' then something is wrong with my marriage." Your emotions will fluctuate widely throughout your marriage. Some days you will feel more "in love" than others. This is natural. It is one reason we make marriage covenants, rather than just relying on our feelings to keep us together from day to day. The exciting feelings of being in love propel you into marriage. They are like the ignition that launches a rocket into space. Then a different kind of love

begins to develop—a strong, warm, companionable feeling that sustains you over time. Yet even this more enduring love can be peppered with times of disagreement and moments of frustration. Unfortunately, you can only marry an imperfect human being, and that's all you can bring to the marriage as well. As you nurture your partner's well-being and the well-being of your relationship, the romance you feel at first can deepen and grow into a mature and lasting love.

As children join your union, you will realize more than ever that life is no longer just about you and your personal fulfillment. The marriage now has a larger purpose and meaning—to create a place where children can thrive. You and your husband will each need to give up some of your own wishes and preferences for the greater good of your family. But it is in doing this—with God as your partner—that you will find the greatest fulfillment of all.

And it came to pass that we lived after the manner of happiness.

—2 Nephi 5:27

A Different Approach

Irene Ericksen

As a single twenty-four-year-old woman, I moved to Salt Lake City to take an exciting new job in the business world. At the time, I was not a Latter-day Saint, and by that point in my life I had dated quite a lot. I met a group of single professionals in Salt Lake and found myself going out with a couple of young professional men.

Then, sixteen months after moving to Salt Lake City and just two weeks short of my twenty-sixth birthday, I became a Latter-day Saint. In the non-LDS world, most of the people my age were still single, and it had felt quite normal to not yet be married. But with my baptism I was surprised to discover that many of the LDS women my age were already married and, more important, most of the LDS young men in my age range were, too.

Before my conversion, my education and my career had been my first priorities. Now marriage began to look more important and appealing. But ironically, I was now in a population where my prospects for marriage were reduced—and increasingly so with each passing year. As a graduate student, I was attending a student ward where most of the men were younger than I was. I dated a few of them briefly, but they did not seem to be looking for someone like me.

After a year of this, I became discouraged. I remember praying for guidance and, after pouring out my heart, getting up from my knees with the answer that it would be better to remain single than to marry someone not suited to me or to marry someone who was not a committed Latter-day Saint. I had made such a dramatic change in converting to the Church that it seemed senseless to even consider uniting with someone who did not share that commitment.

At this same time, I made a decision to change my approach to dating. I saw that in the past I had sometimes been my own worst enemy in romantic relationships. I had been too quick to become emotionally and physically close to the young men I had dated. I had pursued the modern woman's approach to relationships—"I give myself to you heart and soul without any commitment and then wait for you to give yourself to me"—and it had backfired on me every time. Now I decided to try romantic relationships the old-fashioned way. I would wait for the man to commit to and sacrifice for me first before I would invest my feelings or be physically affectionate.

Shortly after making this new resolve, I took a job opportunity that came my way, and there I met Dave. Dave was working part time in my new office, while he was finishing his Ph.D. He was very good looking in an understated way, obviously smart, going somewhere in his life, and a committed Latter-day Saint. And, amazingly, he was twenty-seven and single. But I was not swept off my feet, and he was not bowled over by me. We were just friends at the office.

Gradually, our contact away from the office began to increase. Dave started a singles' study group and invited my LDS roommates and me to join. He called to see if anyone from our apartment wanted to go on a drive to Park City. He and some friends invited our apartment to go play tennis, and it seemed natural for the group to go for pizza and a movie afterward. Then the two of us ended up spending a rainy afternoon driving around looking at old restored houses and becoming better acquainted.

But Dave and I were not "dating." We were just friends who enjoyed each other's company. We enjoyed talking on the telephone and discussing issues of importance in the study-group meetings. And the more we talked, the more I liked him. We continued "not dating" from January through July, and during all of this time the only physical contact we had was holding hands once—when he helped me climb over some rocks on a hike.

Why was he so standoffish? Unknown to me, Dave had also decided to take a new approach to dating. At twenty-seven, he felt like he had dated every single girl between Bountiful and Provo, and it was time to try something different. He had resolved to look harder at what was on the inside than what was on the outside of any girl who sparked his interest. He would get to know the person on the inside before making physical contact with the person on the outside. So there we were, two twenty-seven-year-olds who had done our share of casual kissing, suddenly acting shy and prudish and discovering each other without even holding hands.

The ending, of course, is a happy one. Early in August, Dave put his arm around me and we had our first kiss. Soon after, he started talking about a long-term relationship, and I knew that I was in love, but I waited for more commitment before expressing those feelings. By mid-August Dave began talking about marriage, and we had a decision to make. Having had my heart broken once before, I was fearful of taking that step. Yet I felt reassured that Dave knew who I was and loved the real me. I knew, too, that he was more than the fun and charm I found so irresistible. I knew he was a person of depth, good judgment, and a good heart, who also had a sound testimony of the gospel.

With such an enormous decision before me, I pleaded in prayer for direction. Should I marry this man? Was he "the one," or was there someone else out there in God's plan for me? The answer I received was a little different from what I expected. The Spirit whispered to me that if I did not marry Dave, there would be others I could fall in love with, but that this man was the best opportunity I would have for a happy marriage. This understanding calmed my fears, and we were soon engaged. Even after becoming engaged, we set boundaries together for our physical relationship to keep our passions under control and our focus on knowing the other as a person.

Following this different approach gave Dave and me a different—and much happier—result than we had had in any of our other relationships. We have been married now for twenty years, and the inspiration that guided me to marry Dave has been validated over and over. As I look back, I am grateful that the way we developed our relationship—keeping our distance physically so that we could get to know each other personally—helped lay a strong foundation for our marriage that has blessed us ever since.

IRENE ERICKSEN GREW UP IN PHOENIX, ARIZONA, AND WENT TO COLLEGE IN OREGON BEFORE MOVING TO SALT LAKE CITY, WHERE SHE RECEIVED A MASTER'S DEGREE IN COUNSELING AT THE UNIVERSITY OF UTAH. SHE CURRENTLY DOES SOME FREE-LANCE WORK OUT OF HER HOME, SERVES AS TEACHER IMPROVEMENT COORDINATOR IN HER WARD, AND ENJOYS CLASSIC LITERATURE, LUNCH WITH FRIENDS, AND SUPPORTING HER HUSBAND AND TWO SONS IN THEIR MANY ACTIVITIES.

See that ye bridle all your passions, that ye may be filled with love.

—Alma 38:12

chapter 8

THE MISSION CALLED
MOTHERHOOD

Children need sunlight. They need happiness. They need

love and nurture. They need kindness and refreshment and affection.

Every home . . . can provide an environment of love

which will be an environment of salvation.

—Gordon B. Hinckley (*Teachings*, 53)

A prestigious high-tech company has hired you for a very important job. The company, which specializes in artificial intelligence, has just produced a prototype android that can out-perform humans both physically and mentally. Because this wonderful invention will multiply human productivity, it is seen as a great hope for human civilization. But some people argue that programming or mechanical errors could make this android extremely destructive.

Your job is to supervise the programming and software development for this unit. You will make the final decisions about the unit's database and social behavior. You will be accountable for every aspect of the unit's programming. With a generous salary, plush office, and competent support staff, your job is powerful, prestigious, and highly coveted. And it will have a great impact on the future of civilization, for good or ill. Needless to say, you feel highly motivated to give this job your very best.

Very few of us will ever have this kind of job. But every woman who becomes a mother has a mission infinitely more far-reaching, infinitely more soul-satisfying. Without prestige, without salary, at times without acknowledgment, women quietly do the world's most important work—giving and nurturing life.

A Grand vision of Motherhood

The Lord has told us, in one simple, powerful sentence, what life is all about: "This is my work and my glory—to bring to pass the immortality and eternal life of man" (Moses 1:39). In other words, he desires for us to prepare ourselves, and to help those we love prepare themselves, to become godly beings who can live in his presence—in the presence of joy and love—eternally. Women have an irreplaceable part to play in this grand undertaking. We have the privilege of bringing God's children to life physically and nurturing them as they begin their mortal journey. We literally share in his work.

God designed women for this amazing work. Women have been given a specific chemical makeup to help them succeed in the work of mothering. They have also been given other physical, mental, emotional, and spiritual traits that fit them for this work. Whether you raise children of your own or use your mothering skills to nurture other members of the human family in need, mothering is a very central part of your personal mission as a woman.

Of course, this is not quite the perspective you get when you turn on the television. TV sitcoms, advertisements, and news specials are aimed at you, telling you what you should aspire to become—maybe a professional soccer player, an airline pilot, a social worker, a rock climber, or a fashion model. But do they ever relay the message "Be a good mother; nurture others"? Not very often. And while girls throughout their school years are encouraged to prepare for a career, there is often little focus on preparing to be a good mother.

Yet, regardless of the messages of our popular culture, if you become a mother it will be the most challenging, important, and rewarding job you will ever do in your life. Motherhood is one of the great transforming human experiences. That is why it is available to every woman—either in this life or the next.

planning Ahead

If you wanted to be a neurosurgeon, you would probably have been planning and working toward this goal for some years now. You would need to have taken the right courses in college, for example—and to have excelled in them. Unfortunately, we sometimes spend little time planning and working toward the most important work we may ever do—that of being a mother.

As you think about preparing for the mission called motherhood, you probably have some questions. Many of these questions may involve the challenge of balancing motherhood with a career. How should you prepare for these two important—and sometimes conflicting—aspects of your life? What are some of the needs that cause conflict between career and family life?

Family financial needs. Supporting a family on one income can be a great challenge. As the financial needs of families have grown in most countries, so has the percentage of family income that goes to taxes. A family of four today may pay as much as half of its gross income to federal and state taxes, Social Security and Medicare taxes, and property and sales taxes. This leaves a smaller real income with which to pay higher costs of living. And as divorce rates have increased, so has the number of mothers who are their family's sole support.

Women's personal needs. Some women may feel that their talents and education are not being fully used if their full-time work is taking care of home and children. They may also feel bored with housework and stressed by the constant demands of children. And they may feel isolated at home in a society where the sense of community that once existed in neighborhoods has moved to the workplace. They may also miss the sense of personal validation and measurable accomplishment that they once received in their careers.

Children's needs. For optimum development, children need the full-time care and nurture of their mothers. In the first months of life, the infant identifies a center of her world. This center is naturally the mother, with father playing a close second. Infants and young children are stressed when they have to be away from their mothers—their source of security and comfort—for extended periods of time. In addition, good day care appears to be a rare commodity (see Lowry, "Nasty, Brutish & Short," 36–40). Because child-care workers are so poorly paid, the most competent tend to seek more highly paid work. Even a highly paid nanny who comes into your home does not have the commitment or the longevity of the child's own mother. The revolving door of child-care workers serves the emotional needs of young children very poorly (see Vedantam, "Child Aggressiveness Study," *Washington Post*, 19 April 2001, A6). And some studies have connected the occurrence of juvenile crime and mischief to children being home without parental supervision for several hours after school (see Fox, 20 December 1995).

The simple fact is that no one else will care as much about your child as you do, and so no one else will be as motivated as you are to provide her optimum care. You simply cannot pay another person to care as much about your child, or for your child, as you will. And each child needs the security that comes from being cared for by one who would gladly make literally any sacrifice for her well-being.

A Gospel-based Approach

This problem of conflicting financial needs, career goals, and children's needs may seem far in the future. Yet the decisions you make about this conflict will be some of the most important you will make for your own long-term happiness and the well-being of those you will love most. Planning ahead now will help you to have the results you want.

As with each decision you make along the path of your personal mission, your decisions about motherhood and career are unique to you. They will require study, consultation with your husband, and prayer. Here are some suggestions that can help you resolve the conflicts described above and give you confidence that you are on the right path.

Giving your all. Several decades ago, women were told, "You can have it all!" That is, a woman can have a full-time career, a happy husband and happy children, enough "quality time" to spend with them, and time to fill her own needs. A few years later, this motto was modified to "You can have it all—but not all at once."

But a gospel-centered perspective replaces the goal of "having it all" with one of "giving your all." Jesus said, "For whosoever will save his life shall lose it: and whosoever will lose his life for my sake shall find it" (Matthew 16:25). In other words, instead of thinking in terms of "my career," we should think in terms of "my contribution." As you plan your life, begin by asking questions such as "How can I maximize my contribution to God's work, both now and in the future?" or "How can I do the most good in my life?" These questions will make some of your decisions more clear.

For example, if you have the opportunity to marry and have children, you will do the most good by raising your children to be happy, productive, faithful adults. In most cases, you can do this best by caring for your children yourself while they are young. Planning and preparing for this will enable you to avoid sacrificing this greater contribution for a lesser one that you might make in another valuable profession. Then, when your children are older, you can find opportunities to make other contributions.

On the other hand, if you find your family's financial welfare is at risk, your maximum contribution may be to obtain paid employment so that you can strengthen your family financially. And knowing the importance of your children's needs, you can take some of the steps below to minimize the impacts of your employment on your family.

Planning to "work smart." Gain the very best education and skills you can before you have children so that you can "work smart." For example, instead of working eight hours a day for eight dollars an hour, you could work four hours a day for sixteen dollars an hour. Then, if you do need to be employed, you will be able to spend the least possible amount of time away from your children. Your education will also maximize your contribution to God's work by developing your talents and skills so that you have more to give, both in and out of your home.

Choosing wisely. When you are considering a marriage partner, choose someone who is planning to provide for his family and who is working toward that goal. This may make it possible for you to be a full-time homemaker, at the very least while your children are small.

Saving for your mission as a mother. Start a "mission" savings account right now for your mission as a mother. Set aside a certain amount each month so that, when the time comes, you will have this money to help you stay at home with your young children. After you marry, plan your financial commitments (such as your home mortgage) based on your husband's income alone. Be willing to lower your lifestyle expectations and make some financial sacrifices for your children's well-being while they are young.

Mission training. In the Missionary Training Center, full-time missionaries learn skills to help them succeed in the mission field. You can start now to learn the skills you will need for your mission as a mother. Learn to make a monthly spending plan and stick to it. You can learn to cook from scratch, which is much less expensive and much more healthy than buying prepared foods. Learn to repair clothing. Study child development.

Adapting to circumstances. In spite of your careful planning, you may find that you need to work when your children are young. If so, these ideas can help you minimize the impact it will have on your children:

• Work part time and/or flex time.

• Work at home while your children are asleep, or away while their father is at home.

• Work while your children are at school so that you can be at home when they leave for school and when they return from school. President Ezra Taft Benson called this being "at the crossroads."

Creating circles of support. In addition to being the most rewarding, the vital work of being a mother is the most challenging you will ever do. At times it can be stressful and isolating. By lending your support to other women who are mothers—not passing judgment on their employment decisions or their child-rearing techniques, for example—you can help create a supportive, mother-friendly community for yourself and others. Also, by reaching out to friends and neighbors, you can help create supportive connections within your community. In addition, many full-time mothers of young children arrange a time each week when their children are cared for by a good sitter or their father, and the mothers can have some time for themselves away from their children.

Maybe the high-tech job programming the artificially intelligent android still sounds pretty good to you. After all, a robot doesn't require twenty-four-hours-a-day care. It doesn't require you to change your life or give up your professional identity or any of your recreational opportunities. But there's one major difference that you cannot fully appreciate until you experience being a mother: A robot will never love you.

I think that giving a five-year-old . . . a peanut butter and jelly sandwich with a smile is as important as praying beside the bed of a dying man. . . . Mother Teresa thinks so, too. She says: "What we are doing in the slums, maybe you cannot do. What you are doing in the level where you are called—in your family life, in your college life, in your work—we cannot do. But you and we together are doing something beautiful for God."
—Chieko N. Okazaki (*Cat's Cradle*, 185)

THE CENTER OF THEIR UNIVERSE

NENA SLIGHTING

As I was growing up in the Church, my ultimate goal was to be married in the temple and raise an eternal family. At the same time, my parents always stressed the importance of obtaining an education and pursuing a career. This, too, became a part of my vision of the future. I saw a career not just as a way to have personal fulfillment, but as a way to make a significant contribution to my fellowman. I wanted my life to count for something and to magnify my talents. As I grew older, I wondered how I could achieve both of these worthy goals. How would I be able to pursue a career *and* devote my time and energy to a family— all at the same time?

I had fallen in love during my senior year of college and was married shortly after I graduated. After working for a year, I decided to pursue a law degree. I was interested in the legal profession and saw it as a way to contribute to my community. I also felt that a legal career would allow a flexible work schedule and an adequate income if I ever had to become the main provider for our family. But as I eagerly began my law school studies, I still wasn't sure what I would do about the career and family question, whenever it should arise.

We were faced with this decision sooner than we had planned. During my second year of law school, we were blessed with a beautiful baby daughter. Suddenly any doubts about whether I wanted to stay at home and raise a family disappeared. As I sat staring at this glorious bundle entrusted to me by a loving Heavenly Father, I realized I wanted nothing more than to provide a safe haven in which she could grow and be happy. She was now the center of my universe, and I wanted to surround her with all the love and joy that I possibly could. I knew I could not accomplish this if I were also trying to pursue a career in the competitive legal profession. Still, I felt it was important to finish my law degree, so I pushed on to the finish, and by the time I had graduated, our second daughter was on the way. Fellow law students gave me that "Are you insane?" look, but I knew my career aspirations could wait. I felt I would be fulfilling the most important mission at this point in my life by staying at home with my children.

As my baby daughters began to grow and develop, I came to realize how much they needed me, that *I* was the center of *their* universe. I also came to understand that rearing happy, emotionally healthy children of good character was one of the most important—if not *the* most important—contribution I could make to society, given the opportunities before me. And I realized that motherhood was one of the best ways I could magnify my talents, as it exercised and stretched them in ways I had not anticipated. I also realized that this is a difficult and personal choice for every mother, and I could understand someone making a different choice than I did.

I now have four children, ranging in age from three to twelve years old, and, yes, there have been times when I have doubted the wisdom of my decision—times when the demands on me as a mother have seemed unending and it has seemed that the only interaction I have is with toddlers. My husband and I have also made real financial sacrifices to enable me to stay home. Where some of my fellow law students at this stage of life are buying large, new two-story homes, we have refinished the basement of our brick bungalow to accommodate the six of us. But as I see how quickly my children are growing and understand the limited time my influence is felt, I am very grateful to have the opportunity to devote my full-time attention to them.

I also know that there are many seasons in life in which to accomplish my goals. My mother, who now has a very successful career, did not begin working until the last of her seven children was in school. I have also taken advantage of rewarding volunteer opportunities that use my professional skills. And I am looking forward to having a career when my children are older; I believe there will be many ways for me to fulfill these aspirations at that time. But for now I am content to be where I am needed and challenged the most.

NENA SLIGHTING VOLUNTEERS AT HER CHILDREN'S SCHOOL AND IS CURRENTLY SERVING ON A STATE-WIDE BOARD RELATED TO CHILDREN'S ISSUES. SHE IS ALSO AN ACHIEVEMENT DAY LEADER IN HER SALT LAKE CITY WARD.

Love as powerful as your mother's for you leaves its own mark.
Not a scar, no visible sign . . . to have been loved so deeply,
even though the person who loved us is gone, will give us
some protection forever. It is in your very skin.
—Albus Dumbledore (in Rowling, *Sorcerer's Stone*, 299)

chapter 9

WILL I EVER BE GOOD ENOUGH?
DEALING WITH FEELINGS
OF INADEQUACY

And now, little children, abide in him;

that, when he shall appear, we may have confidence.

—1 John 2:28

In a poem titled "Almost Perfect," Shel Silverstein tells the funny-sad story of Mary Hume. As a seven year old, she is disappointed with her birthday party decorations because they are *not quite* the right color. Growing older, she keeps looking for perfection in a not-quite-perfect world. As a young woman, she refuses a suitor because he squeezes her a little too tightly. Still later, as a schoolteacher, she finds fault with her students for their less-than-perfect penmanship. Mary never quite finds the way to be happy because those around her are *not quite* perfect (see *A Light in the Attic*, 163).

Many women struggle, at least some of the time, with the feeling that, no matter how hard they try, *they* can never be good enough—*almost* good enough . . . *but not quite*. Where do these feelings of inadequacy come from, and how can we overcome them?

The perfection Trap

Perhaps nothing can make us feel so inadequate as the idea that we always need to be perfect. When we see the word *perfect* in the scriptures, we may think it means "without flaw." Often we go even further, thinking it means "having every good attribute in the highest degree." Applying this concept to ourselves—or, rather, *mis*applying it—we may think as follows:

"Besides not making any mistakes, I must also be incredibly athletic, artistic, bright, beautiful, clever, creative, domestic, disciplined . . ." and on and on through the alphabet of desirable attributes. Then, realizing that we not only make mistakes but also that we lack many good traits, we are haunted by the feeling that we don't measure up—in God's eyes or in our own.

But could the Savior really want us to feel this kind of

anxious perfectionism when he asks us to "be perfect"? Whenever you encounter the word *perfect* in the scriptures, look for a footnote to find a truer perspective. There you'll find that the original Hebrew word for *perfect* doesn't mean flawless. It means whole, balanced, complete, and having integrity. So the Savior is not telling us, "You must not make any mistakes." Instead, he seems to be telling us to seek a balanced wholeness, a harmonious integrity in our actions and attitudes.

Nor has the Lord ever intended for any one of us to have every single gift or talent. "For all have not every gift given unto them; . . . to some is given one, and to some is given another, that all may be profited thereby" (D&C 46:11–12). In other words, we all contribute the gifts we have to others. In this way, we are complete or perfect as a whole group, not as individuals. "Also [the Church] hath need of every member, that all may be edified together" (D&C 84:110).

your Body: a gift suited to your mission

A common focus of our self-criticism as women is our physical appearance. How many of your friends are perfectly happy with their current weight? In our society today, girls and young women are seeking a body type that is something like that of an extremely skinny pre-adolescent—with unusually large breasts. Often, they starve themselves to attain it. Sometimes they even resort to surgery. In the process, they come to see their bodies as the enemy—an obstacle to their happiness—and food as a forbidden temptation.

Yet striving to achieve this ideal body is doomed to failure for most women. The head of a major modeling agency once estimated that only about one out of ten thousand women has the body type the fashion world is looking for. It is not just coincidental that the beauty "industry"—which is in the business of selling you products—holds up almost impossible ideals of physical beauty. The harder the "ideal" is to achieve, the more products you will need to buy to try to achieve it. So by holding up virtually unattainable models of beauty, the fashion industry creates an endless market for their "beauty-enhancing" products. Thus women spend huge amounts of time, energy, and money seeking ideals in dress, hair, and makeup. All this, of course, comes at the expense of the emotional, spiritual, and physical well-being of young women.

Sometimes the cost—as in the case of eating disorders—is the life of the young woman. In many times and places, it has meant physical abuse. In China, generations of young girls had their feet broken and bound to fit an impossibly small ideal. European women of past centuries had themselves laced so tightly into their corsets that they couldn't breathe and often fainted, all for the sake of a pencil-thin waistline. In some African countries today, naturally slender girls intentionally overeat to achieve a heavier ideal body type.

God made no mistakes when he designed women's bodies. In fact, our bodies are designed after a divine model. "So God created man in his own image, in the image of God created he him; male and female created he them" (Genesis 1:27). And our bodies are perfectly fitted to help us succeed in our earthly missions. God did not design our legs to be model-slender, but to be strong. He gave us hips that are proportioned perfectly for child-bearing. He gave us a layer of fat beneath our skin that makes our bodies unfashionably soft, but makes us physically hardy and enables us to softly cradle a child. Understanding the purpose of our bodies, we can gratefully accept them as the valuable gifts they are.

Just as we would want to take good care of any valuable gift, we need to take good care of our bodies. This includes grooming and dressing ourselves modestly and attractively. We do look and feel our best when we are well-groomed and well-dressed. And our bodies serve us best when we maintain a healthy weight and physical fitness. But your genetic makeup plays a part in determining your weight and body size. So you should strive to maintain *your* optimum weight, not someone else's. When we learn to accept our bodies, we can achieve greater peace in our lives. This peace is reflected outwardly, which in turn makes us beautiful.

If You're Not Dating . . .

While dating can be challenging in many ways, *not* dating can make you feel truly inadequate. ("What am I, chopped liver?") You probably *know* very well that your worth doesn't depend on whether a young man is showing interest in you at a given moment, but it's hard not to *feel* a little demoralized when that's not happening. You might be shy or lacking in social confidence. Maybe you live in an area where there are few eligible men to date. Or maybe the men you do know seem to have unrealistic expectations about women, looking for a standard of beauty that is hard to measure up to. Or maybe the men in your social circle don't seem to want to get beyond "hanging out" with a group.

While you cannot control some of these realities, you can put yourself in situations where you can interact with quality young men on more than a surface level. Young Single Adult activities, school classes and clubs, and serving together in volunteer and church activities can all offer this kind of opportunity to get acquainted.

But finally, maintaining your sense of self when you wish you were dating becomes a matter of faith—faith in your inherent value as a person and as a daughter of God, faith in God's plan for you, and faith in your ability to have a great life now *and* in the years to come, whatever they may bring.

ready, set, compete!

Throughout her teenage years, Laura worked hard to excel in basketball. When she was finally named to the all-state team, she was puzzled when her teammates not only didn't congratulate her but also stopped passing her the ball in their games.

Do you ever feel that life is a relentless race that you need to finish first? When you do succeed, do others seem jealous of your success? Does the success of others ever make *you* feel envious or insecure?

In *Through the Looking-Glass*, Alice in Wonderland meets Tweedledum and Tweedledee, an absurdly combative set of twins who slow down her progress. Most young women have to deal with an equally contentious set of twins: Competing and Comparing. The world we live in has never been more competitive. If you want to go to a prestigious university, you probably know how difficult it is to be selected for a limited number of available spots. Competition is based on a limited supply of some desirable good—a limited number of slots on a school sports team, for example. And you must beat out other people who are trying to get the same thing.

Unfortunately, in our world, competition is often overused. For example, when Elizabeth was five, her kindergarten teacher required her class to enter a school art show. Elizabeth loved to paint and draw, and she drew a beautiful underwater scene, complete with mermaid. When her picture was not chosen as a "winner," she told her mother sadly, "I guess I'm not a good artist, after all." The next year, she felt insecure and didn't want to take part in the contest. She had learned the false idea that only a select few pictures could be "good" and that she would need to beat others out to gain a reward that was in short supply.

But God's world is one of abundance, not scarcity. He has plenty of love to go around to every one of his children. He has plenty of joy for all of their accomplishments. He has plenty of approval for each of their efforts. With him, we do not need to strive for any "honor roll" or "top ten" or "varsity team." He glories in every single bit of our progress, regardless of how it compares with anyone else's. In our lives, there are many areas where we *do* have to compete with others. But we never have to compete with anyone else to be "good enough" for God's love.

The habit of continually comparing ourselves with others is not an easy one to break. For example, when you walk into a room of other young women, do you ever scan the group and compare yourself to see if you look as good as they do? To start, you might first try avoiding activities that you know will make you feel like you are losing out. If looking at fashion magazines makes you feel dissatisfied with your own body, wardrobe, or lifestyle, for example, you could change your reading habits. Look for friends who seem secure and who don't tear down others who seem to be succeeding.

On a deeper level, we can pray to feel at peace with our own abilities and accomplishments. We can pray to feel secure in God's unconditional love, knowing that he does not require us to beat anyone out for his approval. Then try to see others as he sees them. This will help us to be happy for other people's successes, knowing that they do not diminish our own.

Losses, Defeats, and Mistakes

By the time Kate turned twenty-five, she felt demoralized by some serious disappointments she had suffered. She had been engaged several times, only to have each engagement end in heartache and sorrow. Feeling inadequate and discouraged, she wondered whether her life would ever "work out," or if she would just continue having one difficult setback after another.

One of the greatest life skills you can acquire is the ability to endure defeats without being defeated by them. At this stage, many parts of your life are not yet worked out. And you are in the process of learning many important lessons—some of them through hard experience. But God does not intend for you to be defeated. In fact, he intends for even the most devastating experience to contribute to your eventual triumph. As the Lord told the Prophet Joseph Smith, after listing the most horrific difficulties, "all these things shall give thee experience, and shall be for thy good" (D&C 122:7). He also told the Prophet that "all things shall work together for good to them that walk uprightly" (D&C 100:15). In other words, if we continue to be faithful, *any* setback, however severe, is only temporary.

The Perfect Love of Christ

Have you ever doubted that you can be good enough for the celestial kingdom or that you are good enough to be acceptable to the Lord now? This is something like the little girl who was afraid to go to kindergarten because she didn't know how to read yet. "Of course you can't read yet," her mother told her.

"That is the reason you need to go to kindergarten. Kindergarten is the place you will start learning how to read."

Likewise, we sometimes think that we can come unto the Lord only when we have become perfect on our own *first*. But notice the order in the following verse: "Come unto Christ, and [then] be perfected in him" (Moroni 10:32). In other words, of course you aren't perfect yet. That is the reason you need to come unto Christ. Christ is the very One—and the only One—whose perfect love can help you become whole and happy—or, in other words, perfect. But we can become whole only when we come unto him *first*, with all our imperfections.

Sometimes, too, we have the mistaken idea that salvation is something we earn by our own efforts, rather than a divine gift. Of course, the way we live *is* important, because the Lord's commandments are his rules of happiness; by either living them or ignoring them, we move closer to or further away from God and his influence and goodness. But none of us can be good enough by our own efforts to "earn" eternal life. We must do our best, but it is the perfect love of the Savior, through his atoning sacrifice, that makes up the difference between where our efforts can take us and eternal life.

On our own, we can never reach perfection—no matter how hard we try. But this is part of the plan. We are to rely on the Lord's perfection, not our own. His perfect love is the only cure for the mental torment of perfectionism. "Perfect love [which is *his* love] casteth out fear" (1 John 4:18).

No one of us is less treasured or cherished of God than another. . . .

He loves each of us—insecurities, anxieties, self-image, and all.

—Jeffrey R. Holland ("The Other Prodigal,"

Ensign, May 2002, 64)

Heavenly Father, I Don't Know What to Say

Cynthia Bourne

I was just twenty-five when I became single again. After a two-year struggle with cancer, my husband had died, leaving me a widow with three very young daughters. I was blessed to have a supportive extended family, including a compassionate mother and a father, who was very good at helping me count my blessings. Still, there were times when all I could think of were my challenges.

Several years after my husband's death, feelings of inadequacy and self-doubt began to overtake me. One evening I was feeling particularly discouraged and overwhelmed. I tried to fight feelings of worthlessness and depression, but heaviness and darkness prevailed. After my children were in bed for the night, I sat in a dark room looking out the window at a dark sky, my surroundings reflecting my mood. I pondered my life, my fears, my anxiety, and my feelings of complete inadequacy. No one knew what I was going through. No one could possibly know how I felt.

As I sank deeper into despair, I knew that I should get on my knees and ask for help from my Heavenly Father. In the past, I had received great comfort through prayer. I had even experienced "heavenly hugs"—sacred prayerful moments that gave me the strength to face another day. But on this night I could barely remember how it felt to feel close to the Lord.

The faint memory was in my head but not in my heart. I did not want to pray. For a very long time I wrestled with the idea of saying a prayer.

Finally, out of sheer determination not to let darkness overcome me, I knelt down. The first words that came out of my mouth were, "Heavenly Father, I don't know what to say." I continued pouring out my heart to the Lord vocally. I told him every emotion I was feeling and why. Desperate to talk to someone who could understand me and my life, I confessed every weakness, every fear, every sin, every mistake I could think of.

The feelings that followed amazed me. I knew that the Lord was listening. I felt perfect friendship. I felt his love and acceptance for me at that very moment, "notwithstanding my weakness" (2 Nephi 33:11). Along with that acceptance, I felt encouragement to do more, to try harder, to progress and "press forward." And I felt an overwhelming joy that, with the Lord's help, I could. My heart began to turn to others as I prayed. My prayer even progressed to the point that I could pray sincerely for individuals who had caused me to feel pain. I prayed for relationships to improve, for forgiveness and understanding to heal broken hearts.

I was still kneeling in a dark room, but the room felt full of light. I did not want to close my prayer because I did not want these feelings of love and strength to go away. Quickly I found paper and pencil and began to write down instructions that I felt were very specific for me, instructions that would help me to fight my feelings of being overwhelmed and inadequate. Then I reluctantly closed my prayer.

Later, as I studied the notes I made during my prayer, I realized gratefully that I had been receiving these same instructions my whole life. "Sincerely pray and study the scriptures daily. Keep a journal. Make time for temple work. Tithing and fast offerings are a privilege. Don't let anger drive the Spirit away. Don't run faster than you are able. Keep your covenants and my commandments." The Lord wanted me to succeed, and I have found joy and power by just following these simple instructions. Now when I struggle with self-doubt, I read this wonderful verse: "Cast your mind upon the night that you cried unto me in your heart. . . . Did I not speak peace to your mind . . . ? What greater witness can you have than from God?" (D&C 6:22–23).

No matter what, never let the adversary convince you not to pray. He knows the strength that you can receive in your most desperate, most discouraging moments. The Lord loves you for who you are right now. Ask him. He is eager for you to feel his love and acceptance. It is then that he can encourage you along the path to what he knows you can become.

CYNTHIA BOURNE MARRIED AGAIN IN 1987, AND SHE AND HER HUSBAND, HAL BOURNE, HAVE ELEVEN CHILDREN. A STAKE RELIEF SOCIETY PRESIDENT IN SALT LAKE CITY, SHE ENJOYS MOUNTAIN BIKING, SKIING, AND RUNNING MARATHONS.

For I know the thoughts that I think toward you, saith the Lord,
thoughts of peace, and not of evil, to give you an expected end.
Then shall ye call upon me, and ye shall go and pray unto me,
and I will hearken unto you. And ye shall seek me, and find me,
when ye shall search for me with all your heart.

—Jeremiah 29:11–13

chapter 10

WHERE DO I FIT
IN THE CHURCH?

Now therefore ye are no more strangers and foreigners,
but fellowcitizens with the saints, and of the household of God.
—Ephesians 2:19

I f you grew up as a Latter-day Saint, you probably always knew just where you fit in the Church. When you were three, you sat on the first row in Primary, just like all the other Sunbeams. Later on, you became a Beehive, a Mia Maid, and a Laurel with all the other twelve- through seventeen-year-old girls. You had regular Young Women activities on a certain night of the week. And your school days may have included an hour of seminary class.

But now you may wonder, "Where exactly do I fit in at church?" For one thing, your peer group has probably gone in many different directions. Some have gone away to college. Several may already be engaged or even married. Unless you are in a student ward, you may feel out of place in a ward made up mostly of older people, families, and younger children.

"as sisters in zion"

One of the big changes in your church experience is the transition from Young Women to Relief Society. In Relief Society, most of the women are not only older, but in situations quite different from yours. The lessons may seem to apply mostly to their needs and concerns. How can you find a comfortable place in the sisterhood of Relief Society?

You may be surprised to learn that the very first Relief Society in Nauvoo included not only a prophet's wife, but three teenagers and six unmarried women. Despite very different backgrounds, the twenty women in that original group shared a common faith and a determination to express that faith through service. The cause that first united them was sewing shirts for the workers building the Nauvoo Temple.

What can unite you with the women in your Relief Society who may seem so different from you? Faith in the gospel, certainly. But what about friendship? You may find women of very different ages and situations who share your interests and feelings. Also, you will find that older women, who have experienced much of life, are often accepting and nonjudgmental of others, and as you look beyond the surface, you may find a real kindred spirit or two among them. You may also find women who are role models and even mentors for you.

Relief Society also provides a structure through which you can have opportunities to serve—a fundamental need at this and every other stage of life. Visiting teaching will also give you opportunities to know other women one-on-one. Even if you do not become best friends with those you visit and those who visit you, visiting teaching will help you find familiar, friendly faces when you walk into Relief Society.

As a younger member, you can provide the energy and enthusiasm that your Relief Society needs. You can learn from the wisdom and experience of the older members, and they can benefit from your perspective as well. Being part of a society of benevolent women can bring rich blessings to you now and throughout your life.

staying connected

Taking care of your own spiritual well-being includes not only staying connected with your Heavenly Father through prayer and study but also staying connected with his church. You may have several types of wards to choose from—a student ward, a singles ward, or a resident (family) ward. Though there are some differences in each of these wards, there will be opportunities to serve, things to learn, and friends to make. If you do have these options, prayerfully choose the ward that seems to best fit your needs.

It may take some extra effort on your part at this phase of your life to keep connected to your ward family. Here are some ideas that can help, especially in a resident ward:

• Attend your meetings consistently in your own ward. If you spend week after week "shopping around" or attending missionary farewells in other wards, you may begin to feel like a visitor in your own ward.

• Let your bishopric know that you are willing to serve in a church calling. And when you do receive a calling, magnify it faithfully. Nothing will help you feel connected to others like serving them and serving with them.

• Make contact with families. Attend church activities and take opportunities to socialize with families in your ward. You can also look for opportunities to serve others in different situations—visiting an elderly ward member or tutoring a child struggling with schoolwork. You might even sometimes sit with a family that appears to need another loving adult to help with the children.

• When you need a priesthood blessing, contact your home teachers or a bishopric member.

• Reach out to those in your own age group. Attend stake young adult activities, and offer rides to others. By taking the first step and extending friendly gestures to others, you can help others stay connected to the Church, too.

As a young adult woman, you may or may not have an active priesthood holder in your home. If you do not, you may have to make a little extra effort to have access to priesthood blessings and counsel. Your bishop and home teachers are there to help provide this, but may not offer to help unless you ask for it. The priesthood leadership role that the Lord has given to worthy men is a great blessing to women. It is parallel to the great responsibilities given to women in the family and the Church. Popular culture would say that in order for men and women to be equal they have to be the same. However, the gospel teaches that men and women are created equal with some important differences. As President Spencer W. Kimball said, "Our roles and assignments differ. These are eternal differences—with women being given many tremendous responsibilities of motherhood and sisterhood and men the tremendous responsibilities of fatherhood and the priesthood—but the man is not without the woman nor the woman without the man in the Lord (1 Corinthians 11:11)" (My Beloved Sisters, 37).

your faith: a work in progress

As your faith in God and your testimony of his church are maturing, questions and doubts will inevitably arise. And you may feel alone with your doubts.

When you were a younger girl, did your legs ever ache as you lay in bed at night? During times of rapid growth, "growing pains" are natural. Your spirit can sometimes experience growing pains, too. And like the pains in your legs, these spiritual growing pains are not a cause for alarm. Quite the opposite— they show that your spirit is in a period of rapid growth.

But sometimes, because you no longer have the simple, childlike faith you once had, you may fear that you are losing your testimony. You may long for the time when you felt surer of God's reality. As a child you may have confidently said, "I know the Church is true." Right now, you may not always feel quite so sure—at least not sure in the same way you once did.

But do not worry. As your child's faith and testimony are stretching and growing into an adult's, you will naturally experience spiritual growing pains. Life's complexities will challenge your faith—often very painfully. But if you will always keep seeking the Lord's guidance, you will find that his truths are adequate to meet those complexities.

Picture a small pinprick of light on a background of darkness. The light represents the things you know, the darkness the things you don't. And where the light meets the dark, you experience uncertainty. As you get older, the circle of light greatly expands. But so does the perimeter where the light meets the darkness. As you learn more and more, you become more and more aware of all that you don't know. This may feel scary at first. But you can trust that the One who has a complete picture and sees no darkness at all will *never* forsake you. And as you grow, your own understanding will become more and more complete, more "perfect" in the scriptural sense.

When you have questions and doubts, don't fear them. But do entertain them with an attitude of faith. You may want to discuss your questions with a bishop or someone else you respect. Then keep feeding your faith through prayer, searching the scriptures, and participating in the Church. Some of your answers will come soon, some much later. Be patient with your own spiritual growth, and you will find that, in the Lord's own words, "[She] that receiveth light, and continueth in God, receiveth more light; and that light groweth brighter and brighter until the perfect day" (D&C 50:24).

It may take extra effort to stay close to the Church during

your young adult years. But by doing so, you will find that you have much to give—and much to gain.

And the multitude of them that believed
were of one heart and of one soul.
—Acts 4:32

Lighting the Way

THE PLACE WHERE HE CAN BE FOUND

SUSAN HAINSWORTH

Throughout my life I have had the opportunity of living in very diverse branches and wards of the Church. As a teenager, I lived in a small town in western Kentucky. Our branch was so small that we met in the local Seventh-day Adventist building, and my brothers and I were the only church members at our high school. At college, I attended student wards filled with strong Latter-day Saints all close to my own age and circumstance. Now, as an unmarried woman with no children, I attend a ward made up almost completely of married couples with children. There have been challenges inherent in each of these circumstances, but I have loved being active in the Church wherever I have been.

How could this be so? It is because The Church of Jesus Christ of Latter-day Saints is the place where the Savior can be found. I love him with my whole heart and know that only this church teaches the complete truth about him and provides the sacred ordinances that bind our souls to him. Knowing this, I have been able to fit into the Church, no matter what my personal circumstance or the characteristics of my branch or ward.

Soon after I graduated from college, I went with several friends on a backpacking trip to a red rock canyon in southern Utah. One afternoon I hiked by myself to a small side canyon, where a stream of water made everything around me green and lush. Flowers and ferns grew in abundance, while a short distance away the rock was barren and dry. In this beautiful place, I felt close to the Lord. I felt his Spirit whisper to me that he was as necessary to my life as this water was to the beauty surrounding me. My life would never become all that it could be if I did not remain completely connected to the Savior, the source of life and light and joy.

My desire to remain close to the Savior and his church has not remained untested. Sometimes I have had to hang on tightly to my faith and continue to be active even when things seemed to be going wrong in my life or when belonging to the Church did not seem to be solving my problems.

Some years ago, there was a period of great difficulty in my life when I was not sure that God was guiding me. I felt left alone and could not see how things would work out or get better. During this time, I tried as hard as I could to focus my faith on the Savior. I hoped and prayed that he was still there, even though I could not see that he loved me. I continued to attend my meetings, to read the scriptures, to fulfill my Church callings, and to go to the temple. Many months passed before I could look back at this time and see that, at the very time when the Savior had seemed far away, blessings of immense and long-lasting importance had dropped quietly one by one into my life, creating a pattern of love and beauty and happiness that spoke clearly to me of his love and care. This experience strengthened my testimony that the Savior, Jesus Christ, will always guide and bless me, and that this is his church.

I have tried to approach my activity in the Church as a true disciple of the Savior. When I have been given a church assignment or felt uncomfortable in a church class or activity,

I have asked myself, "How would a disciple of Jesus Christ act in this situation?" This question has led me to seek out those who might need my help, rather than waiting for others to seek me out. It has led me to see assignments as ways to bless others, rather than as inconveniences. This attitude of discipleship has made it much easier for me to fit in when I might otherwise have felt out of place.

I believe that the Church needs the talents I have to offer, and I know that I need all the blessings provided by the Church. I have found wonderful friends, opportunities to grow and serve, spiritual light and power, and most important, the wonderful love of the Savior, Jesus Christ—all in his true church.

SUSAN HAINSWORTH IS AN EDITOR FOR THE LDS CURRICULUM DEPARTMENT AND A FIBER ARTIST WHO ENJOYS CREATING BEAUTIFUL THINGS THROUGH WEAVING, KNITTING, AND QUILTING. SHE SERVES IN THE PRIMARY PRESIDENCY OF HER WARD IN CENTERVILLE, UTAH.

Every one that thirsteth, come ye to the waters.

—Isaiah 55:1

conclusion

A MISSION CALL

God our strength will be;
press forward ever, called to serve our King.
—*Hymns*, no. 249

About six hundred years ago, there lived a young woman in a small village. Her country had been under siege for decades, her town often raided by enemies from across the border. The king was in hiding, and his armies were demoralized. It seemed inevitable that the country would be conquered and laid waste by its enemies.

Then one day, this seventeen-year-old girl, who could neither read nor write and who had spent her life learning to spin and sew and tend the flocks, felt inspired by God to do something to save her nation.

At first she resisted the idea. After all, she was only a young girl. But her feelings were so strong that she finally requested a horse and a suit of armor and went to the king, explaining that God had given her a mission to save France. By the time she died at age nineteen, Joan of Arc had led the French army to victory, restored the king to the throne, and set in motion forces that liberated France from the English and established it as a sovereign nation and a major European power.

Just over two thousand years ago, somewhere in the western hemisphere, two civilizations were engaged in mortal conflict. The aggressors were winning when a unique band of young men came forward and offered to place themselves in the forefront of the battle. They were young and inexperienced, but fearless and full of faith. These young men—the two thousand stripling warriors—played a crucial role in many battles, helping to turn the tide of the war, driving the enemy from their land.

It might be tempting to say that these dramatic incidents are historical flukes. It might be tempting to say that Joan of Arc and the stripling warriors are extremely unusual individuals who come along only once every several hundred years. This may be true. *And* it may also be true that *you* are part of an army of just such individuals. There are more than a million young adult Latter-day Saint women throughout the world today. You and your LDS sisters across the globe are the daughters of Helaman of the twenty-first century. Like Queen Esther, Joan of Arc, and the stripling warriors, you are uniquely positioned and needed to save your people and your civilization.

• If *you* don't exert your civilizing influence on our degenerating society, who will?

• If *you* don't fight the sexual exploitation of young women in our culture, who will?

• If *you* don't reject provocative clothing and degrading entertainment, who will?

• If *you* don't make rearing happy children a top priority, who will?

While your personal mission is probably not on the same scale as that of Joan of Arc, be assured that wherever it can be felt, your influence is badly needed.

A New Vision

The world presents several pictures of what it means to be a successful and valued woman. One cultural stereotype tells you to make homemade bread, can fruit, make crafts, have a beautiful home and strive for gracious living. Another worldly stereotype tells you to live for yourself, for your career, for your own entertainment and pleasure, and for sex and romance.

What is your vision of the woman the Lord wants you to be?

In 1869, in the new and growing settlements of the Salt Lake Valley, President Brigham Young saw a challenge to the young women of his day, some of whom were his own daughters. They were being increasingly drawn to the popular fashions and morals of the world, and they were losing sight of their purpose and priorities as daughters of God. President Young established an organization for young women to help them resist this pull, separate themselves from worldly influences, and focus on their mission as female followers of Christ. He called it "The Young Ladies Retrenchment Society." The word *retrench* means to cut back or pull back from. At that time, President Young said, "I am weary of the manner in which our [young] women seek to outdo each other in all the foolish fashions of the world." He encouraged the society's first members to "vote to retrench in your dress, . . . in your speech, . . . and light-mindedness of thought. Retrench in everything that is not good and beautiful . . . to live so that you may be truly happy in this life and the life to come" (in Gates, *The Life Story of Brigham Young*, 303–6). In other words, he asked them to pull away from the worldly influences that were tempting them.

What would happen if young adult Latter-day Saint women all over the world individually decided to "retrench" from the destructive aspects of worldly culture and join in setting a new standard and a new vision for all young adult women everywhere? And what might that vision be? How about something like this:

This young woman has a sense of personal mission. She asks, "How can I maximize my contribution to God's work at this stage of my life and in the future?" She knows her worth as a daughter of God and knows that she has unique personal gifts and special female strengths that the Lord has given her to magnify in fulfilling her mission. She is willing to support her male counterparts in

magnifying their uniquely male strengths and roles in God's king-
dom. She seeks to be educated, to be self-reliant, and to prepare her-
self in every way for the work God needs her to do.

She sets a new standard in her dress, wearing attractive, modest
clothing. She looks for creative ways to set a new standard in enter-
tainment; she refuses to use her money to support or subsidize the
adversary's campaign material. She is willing to take a stand against
the evil influences around her and is alert for opportunities to do so.

She is proud of the role of mother and homemaker. She is willing
to prepare for it and place it above her own career achievements.
She knows the crucial part she can play as a civilizing force in soci-
ety and that her influence is needed as a doer of good and a leader in
her community. She knows that she has a crucial mission to fulfill,
whether she lives her life as a single or a married women, a mother
of her own children or a mother-er of others' children. She looks for
ways to succor the downtrodden, in her neighborhood and beyond.

Finally, as a follower of the Savior, she strives to be an example
of righteous womanhood, and in a loving and tolerant way to be a
light to young adult women who do not have the blessing of the
gospel to protect them from the all-out attack the adversary has
aimed at them.

In this day, you do not face armies with swords and shields.
But the false messages and evil forces that you face are enemies
just as real and deadly as those faced by heroes of the past.
And, like the enemies of any great cause under siege, they will
not go down without a fight. Together with your Latter-day
Saint sisters, you are needed as part of a great army, a sisterhood standing for truth and defending God's people. As you
respond to his call, you will discover that the Lord does indeed
have a personal mission for you. We pray that you will seek

this mission, that you will find it, and that you will strive to
live it with all your heart.

If there ever were a time when the Lord needed righteous, determined
women who can distinguish between the adversary's deceptions
and the voice of the Lord, it is now.
If there were ever a time when the Lord needed women of integrity and
purity who live in the world but rise above it, it is now.
If there were ever a time when the Lord needed His daughters to be
alert to what is happening in society and to defend the
sanctity of the home and family, it is now. . . .
If there were ever a time when the Lord needed us to have a clear vision
of who we are, where we are, and what is important, it is now.
—Sheri L. Dew (*No Doubt about It*, 233–34)

works cited

Ballard, M. Russell. "'Here Am I, Send Me,'" in *Ye Shall Bear Record of Me: Talks from the 2001 BYU Women's Conference*. Salt Lake City: Deseret Book, 2002.

Benson, Ezra Taft. "To the Young Women of the Church" (pamphlet). Salt Lake City: The Church of Jesus Christ of Latter-day Saints, 1986.

Children's Songbook. Salt Lake City: The Church of Jesus Christ of Latter-day Saints, 1997.

Churchhill, Winston. As quoted by Jeffrey R. Holland, "Sanctify Yourselves," *Ensign*, November 2000.

Dew, Sheri L. *No Doubt about It*. Salt Lake City: Deseret Book, 2002.

Fox, James Allen. Testimony given at a hearing on juvenile drug use before the United States Senate Judiciary Committee. 20 December 1995.

Gates, Susa Young. *The Life Story of Brigham Young*. New York: Macmillan, 1930.

Grimm's Fairy Tales. Stamford, CT: Longmeadow Press, 1987.

Hinckley, Gordon B. "A Prophet's Counsel and Prayer for Youth," *Ensign*, January 2001.

———"God Will Make a Way," *New Era*, January 2002.

———"Stand Strong against the Wiles of the World," *Ensign*, November 1995.

———*Teachings of Gordon B. Hinckley*. Salt Lake City: Deseret Book, 1997.

Holland, Jeffrey R. "The Other Prodigal," *Ensign*, May 2002.

Holland, Patricia T. *A Quiet Heart*. Salt Lake City: Deseret Book, 2000.

Hymns of The Church of Jesus Christ of Latter-day Saints. Salt Lake City: The Church of Jesus Christ of Latter-day Saints, 1985.

Kimball, Spencer W. *Faith Precedes the Miracle*. Salt Lake City: Deseret Book, 1972.

———*My Beloved Sisters*. Salt Lake City: Deseret Book, 1979.

Lewis, C. S. *The Chronicles of Narnia: The Lion, The Witch, and the Wardrobe*. New York: Harper Trophy, 1994.

Lowry, Richard, "Nasty, Brutish & Short," *National Review,* vol. 53, no. 10, 28 May 2001.

Making Melody: Popular Choruses and Hymns. Compiled by Nicholas Arthur Woychuck. Shreveport, La.: Bible Memory Association, 1960, no. 111.

Okazaki, Chieko N. *Cat's Cradle.* Salt Lake City: Bookcraft, 1993.

Packer, Boyd K., "The Father and the Family," *Ensign,* May 1994.

Rowling, J. K. *Harry Potter and the Sorcerer's Stone.* New York: Scholastic, 1999.

Silverstein, Shel. "Almost Perfect," in *A Light in the Attic.* New York: Harper & Row, 1981.

Smith, Joseph. *Teachings of the Prophet Joseph Smith.* Selected by Joseph Fielding Smith. Salt Lake City, Deseret Book, 1970.

Vedantam, Shankar, "Child Aggressiveness Study Cites Day Care," Washington Post, 19 April 2001, A6.

Young, Brigham. *Journal of Discourses (JD),* 26 vols. London: Latter-day Saints' Book Depot, 1854–86.

index